A note regarding the *Psalms* volume of

◆ THE SAINT JOHN'S BIBLE ◆

The Psalms are literally the liturgical song book of ancient Israel. How would one illustrate a song?

To do so is made more complicated by the fact that these songs are laments, coronation hymns, hymns of praise, and odes to wisdom. They also come from a variety of periods and give a sweeping view of Israel's history; locking them into one period with a particular picture would not do them justice. According to Christians, the Psalms also reflect the coming Messiah, Jesus Christ. Moreover, they have been used in Jewish and Christian liturgies for thousands of years with two different, theological emphases.

Through the use of colors, stripes, and shapes this volume weaves the Psalms into a tapestry representing the different threads of the Jewish and Christian history thereby leading the reader and viewer to appreciate the complexity and grandeur of God.

Psalms exemplifies both the creative spirit of *The Saint John's Bible* and the project's ecumenical underpinnings. For centuries, the book of Psalms has been the source of prayer, devotion, and inspiration. As a reminder that the Psalms are sacred songs, the rendering of this book in *The Saint John's Bible* includes visual representations—literally voiceprints—of chants from Benedictine monks running horizontally through the passages. And as a sign of respect for the sacred songs of other traditions, the voiceprints of the monks intersect with similar voiceprints of Jewish, Native American, Muslim, and Taoist chants.

The abstract images found in Psalms encourage a slow and meditative reading, which is the basis of the ancient Christian practice of *lectio divina*, a practice leading the mind, heart, and soul to a greater appreciation of the Word of God.

PSALMS

The Saint John's Bible

Handwritten and Illuminated by Donald Jackson

VERITAS

© 2006
The Order of Saint Benedict
Collegeville, Minnesota 56321
All rights reserved
The Saint John's Bible
Published in Ireland, The United Kingdom
and Europe by Veritas, Ltd.
7/8 Lower Abbey Street, Dublin 1
www.veritas.ie

www.saintjohnsbible.org
www.litpress.org

ISBN 1 85390 833 9

There are 1,150 pages of *The Saint John's Bible* in seven distinct volumes: *Pentateuch, Historical Books, Wisdom Literature, Psalms, Prophets, Gospels and Acts* and *Letters and Revelation.*

In addition, a separate book entitled *Illuminating the Word: The Making of The Saint John's Bible*, by Christopher Calderhead, is available.

Donald Jackson, as Artistic Director, gathered a group of artist-calligraphers and illuminators from around the world. He worked together with them to produce the very best in calligraphy and illumination. They each brought their own skills and perspectives. Their expertise and affection for the art and for *The Saint John's Bible* project contributed to this volume in countless ways.

Artistic Director
Donald Jackson

Artists, Scribes and Designers
Donald Jackson
Vin Godier
Sally Mae Joseph
Brian Simpson

Other members of the Scriptorium team
Mabel Jackson, *Partner*
Rebecca Cherry, *Project Manager*
Sarah Harris, *Studio Assistant*
Sally Sargeant, *Proofreader*

Psalms is divided into five books. The scribes for each are:
Book I: Brian Simpson
Book II: Sally Mae Joseph
Book III: Donald Jackson
Book IV: Donald Jackson
Book V: Sally Mae Joseph

PSALMS

1 HAPPY ARE THOSE WHO DO NOT FOLLOW THE ADVICE OF THE WICKED, OR TAKE THE PATH THAT SINNERS TREAD, OR SIT IN THE SEAT OF SCOFFERS; 2 BUT THEIR DELIGHT IS IN THE LAW OF THE LORD, AND ON HIS LAW THEY MEDITATE DAY AND NIGHT.

3 THEY ARE LIKE TREES PLANTED BY STREAMS OF WATER, WHICH YIELD THEIR FRUIT IN ITS SEASON, AND THEIR LEAVES DO NOT WITHER. IN ALL THAT THEY DO, THEY PROSPER.

4 THE WICKED ARE NOT SO, BUT ARE LIKE CHAFF THAT THE WIND DRIVES AWAY. 5 THEREFORE THE WICKED WILL NOT STAND IN THE JUDGMENT,

NOR
SINNERS
IN THE
CONGREGATION
OF THE
RIGHTEOUS:
6 FOR THE LORD
WATCHES OVER
THE WAY
OF THE
RIGHTEOUS,
BUT THE
WAY OF THE
WICKED
WILL
PERISH.

IV

V

BOOK I

Psalm 2

Why do the nations conspire,
  and the peoples plot in vain?
2 The kings of the earth set themselves,
  and the rulers take counsel together,
  against the LORD and his anointed, saying,
3 "Let us burst their bonds asunder,
  and cast their cords from us."

4 He who sits in the heavens laughs;
  the LORD has them in derision.
5 Then he will speak to them in his wrath,
  and terrify them in his fury, saying,
6 "I have set my king on Zion, my holy hill."

7 I will tell of the decree of the LORD:
  He said to me, "You are my son;
  today I have begotten you.
8 Ask of me, and I will make the nations
    your heritage,
  and the ends of the earth your possession.
9 You shall break them with a rod of iron,
  and dash them in pieces like
    a potter's vessel."

10 Now therefore, O kings, be wise;
  be warned, O rulers of the earth.
11 Serve the LORD with fear,
  with trembling 12 kiss his feet,
  or he will be angry, and you will perish
    in the way;
  for his wrath is quickly kindled.

Happy are all who take refuge in him.

Psalm 1

Happy are those
  who do not follow the advice of the wicked,
  or take the path that sinners tread,
    or sit in the seat of scoffers;
2 but their delight is in the law of the LORD,
  and on his law they meditate day and night.
3 They are like trees
  planted by streams of water,
  which yield their fruit in its season,
  and their leaves do not wither.
  In all that they do, they prosper.

4 The wicked are not so,
  but are like chaff that the wind drives away.
5 Therefore the wicked will not stand
    in the judgment,
  nor sinners in the congregation
    of the righteous;
6 for the LORD watches over the way
    of the righteous,
  but the way of the wicked will perish.

a Cn: Meaning of Heb of
  verses 11b and 12 a is
  uncertain
b Syr: Heb him

v Wisdom
vii Royal
1 Lament

Psalm 3

A Psalm of David,
when he fled from his son Absalom.

O LORD, how many are my foes!
  Many are rising against me;
2 many are saying to me,
  "There is no help for you in God."   Selah

3 But you, O LORD, are a shield around me,
  my glory, and the one who lifts up my head.
4 I cry aloud to the LORD,
  and he answers me from his holy hill.   Selah

5 I lie down and sleep;
  I wake again, for the LORD sustains me.
6 I am not afraid of ten thousands of people

who have set themselves against
me all around.

7 Rise up, O LORD!
Deliver me, O my God!
For you strike all my enemies on the cheek;
you break the teeth of the wicked.

8 Deliverance belongs to the LORD;
may your blessing be on your people!   Selah

Psalm 4

To the leader: with stringed instruments.
A Psalm of David.

Answer me when I call, O God of my right!
You gave me room when I was in distress.
Be gracious to me, and hear my prayer.

2 How long, you people, shall my honor
suffer shame?
How long will you love vain words, and
seek after lies?   Selah
3 But know that the LORD has set apart the
faithful for himself;
the LORD hears when I call to him.

4 When you are disturbed, do not sin;
ponder it on your beds, and be silent.   Selah
5 Offer right sacrifices,
and put your trust in the LORD.

6 There are many who say, "O that we might
see some good!
Let the light of your face shine on us,
O LORD!"
7 You have put gladness in my heart
more than when their grain and
wine abound.

8 I will both lie down and sleep in peace;
for you alone, O LORD, make me lie
down in safety.

Psalm 5

To the leader: for the flutes. A Psalm of David.

Give ear to my words, O LORD;
give heed to my sighing.
2 Listen to the sound of my cry,
my King and my God,
for to you I pray.

3 O LORD, in the morning you hear my voice;
in the morning I plead my case to you,
and watch.

4 For you are not a God who delights
in wickedness;
evil will not sojourn with you.
5 The boastful will not stand before your eyes;
you hate all evildoers.
6 You destroy those who speak lies;
the LORD abhors the bloodthirsty
and deceitful.

7 But I, through the abundance of your
steadfast love,
will enter your house,
I will bow down toward your holy temple
in awe of you.
8 Lead me, O LORD, in your righteousness
because of my enemies;
make your way straight before me.

9 For there is no truth in their mouths;
their hearts are destruction;
their throats are open graves;
they flatter with their tongues.
10 Make them bear their guilt, O God;
let them fall by their own counsels;
because of their many transgressions
cast them out,
for they have rebelled against you.

11 But let all who take refuge in you rejoice;
let them ever sing for joy.
Spread your protection over them,
so that those who love your name
may exult in you.
12 For you bless the righteous, O LORD;
you cover them with favor as with a shield.

Psalm 6

To the leader: with stringed instruments;
according to the Sheminith.
A Psalm of David.

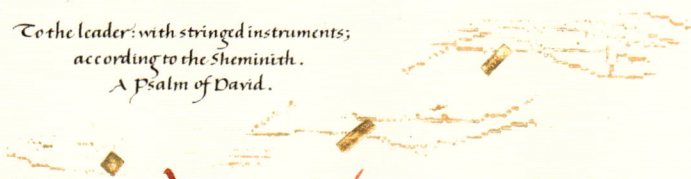

O LORD, do not rebuke me
in your anger,
or discipline me in your wrath.
2 Be gracious to me, O LORD, for
I am languishing;

* Or are angry

I Lament

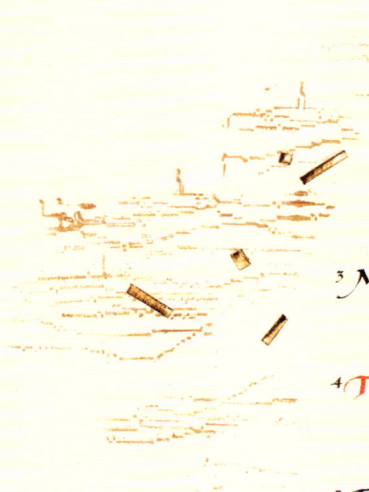

O LORD, heal me, for my bones are
shaking with terror.
3 My soul also is struck with terror;
while you, O LORD – how long?

4 Turn, O LORD, save my life;
deliver me for the sake of your
steadfast love.
5 For in death there is no remembrance of you;
in Sheol who can give you praise?

6 I am weary with my moaning;
every night I flood my bed with tears;
I drench my couch with my weeping.
7 My eyes waste away because of grief;
they grow weak because of all my foes.

8 Depart from me, all you workers of evil,
for the LORD has heard the sound
of my weeping.
9 The LORD has heard my supplication;
the LORD accepts my prayer.
10 All my enemies shall be ashamed and
struck with terror;
they shall turn back, and in a moment
be put to shame.

Psalm 7

A Shiggaion of David, which he sang to the LORD
concerning Cush, a Benjaminite.

O LORD my God, in you I take refuge;
save me from all my pursuers,
and deliver me,
2 or like a lion they will tear me apart;
they will drag me away, with
no one to rescue.

3 O LORD my God, if I have done this,
if there is wrong in my hands,
4 if I have repaid my ally with harm
or plundered my foe without cause,
5 then let the enemy pursue and overtake me,
trample my life to the ground,
and lay my soul in the dust.   Selah

6 Rise up, O LORD, in your anger;
lift yourself up against the fury
of my enemies;
awake, O my God; you have appointed
a judgment.
7 Let the assembly of the peoples be
gathered around you,

and over it take your seat on high.
8 The LORD judges the peoples;
judge me, O LORD, according to
my righteousness
and according to the integrity that is in me.

9 O let the evil of the wicked come to an end,
but establish the righteous,
you who test the minds and hearts,
O righteous God.
10 God is my shield,
who saves the upright in heart.
11 God is a righteous judge,
and a God who has indignation every day.

12 If one does not repent, God will
whet his sword;
he has bent and strung his bow;
13 he has prepared his deadly weapons,
making his arrows fiery shafts.
14 See how they conceive evil,
and are pregnant with mischief,
and bring forth lies.
15 They make a pit, digging it out,
and fall into the hole that they have made.
16 Their mischief returns upon their own heads,
and on their own heads their
violence descends.

17 I will give to the LORD the thanks due to
his righteousness,
and sing praise to the name of the LORD,
the Most High.

Psalm 8

To the leader: according to The Gittith.
A Psalm of David.

O LORD, our Sovereign,
how majestic is your name in all the earth!

You have set your glory above the heavens.
2 Out of the mouths of babes and infants
you have founded a bulwark
because of your foes,
to silence the enemy and the avenger.

3 When I look at your heavens, the work
of your fingers,
the moon and the stars that you
have established;
4 what are human beings that you are
mindful of them,

RSB
Psalm 7:9

d Or awake for me
e Cn: Heb return
f Heb he

I Lament
II Hymn

mortals that you care for them?

5 Yet you have made them a little
    lower than God,[h]
    and crowned them with glory and honor.
6 You have given them dominion over the
    works of your hands;
    you have put all things under their feet,
7 all sheep and oxen,
    and also the beasts of the field,
8 the birds of the air, and the fish of the sea,
    whatever passes along the paths of the seas.

9 O Lord, our Sovereign,
    how majestic is your name in all the earth!

Psalm 9

To the leader: according to Muth-labben.
A Psalm of David.

1 I will give thanks to the Lord with
    my whole heart;
    I will tell of all your wonderful deeds.
2 I will be glad and exalt in you;
    I will sing praise to your name, O Most High.

3 When my enemies turned back,
    they stumbled and perished before you.
4 For you have maintained my just cause;
    you have sat on the throne giving
    righteous judgment.

5 You have rebuked the nations, you have
    destroyed the wicked;
    you have blotted out their name
    forever and ever.
6 The enemies have vanished in
    everlasting ruins;
    their cities you have rooted out;
    the very memory of them has perished.

7 But the Lord sits enthroned forever,
    he has established his throne for judgment.
8 He judges the world with righteousness;
    he judges the peoples with equity.

9 The Lord is a stronghold for the oppressed,
    a stronghold in times of trouble.
10 And those who know your name put
    their trust in you,
    for you, O Lord, have not forsaken
    those who seek you.

11 Sing praises to the Lord, who dwells in Zion.
    Declare his deeds among the peoples.
12 For he who avenges blood is mindful of them;
    he does not forget the cry of the afflicted.

13 Be gracious to me, O Lord.
    See what I suffer from those who hate me;
    you are the one who lifts me up from
    the gates of death,
14 so that I may recount all your praises,
    and, in the gates of daughter Zion,
    rejoice in your deliverance.

15 The nations have sunk in the pit
    that they made;
    in the net that they hid has their own
    foot been caught.
16 The Lord has made himself known,
    he has executed judgment;
    the wicked are snared in the work of
    their own hands. Higgaion. Selah

17 The wicked shall depart to Sheol,
    all the nations that forget God.

18 For the needy shall not always be forgotten,
    nor the hope of the poor perish forever.

19 Rise up, O Lord! Do not let mortals prevail;
    let the nations be judged before you.
20 Put them in fear, O Lord;
    let the nations know that they
    are only human. Selah

Psalm 10

1 Why, O Lord, do you stand far off?
    Why do you hide yourself in
    times of trouble?
2 In arrogance the wicked persecute the poor—
    let them be caught in the schemes
    they have devised.

3 For the wicked boast of the desires
    of their heart,
    those greedy for gain curse and
    renounce the Lord.
4 In the pride of their countenance the wicked
    say, "God will not seek it out";
    all their thoughts are, "There is no God."

a Heb ben adam, lit. son of
man
h Or than the divine beings
or angels: Heb elohim

111 Thanksgiving

⁵ Their ways prosper at all times;
your judgments are on high,
out of their sight;
as for their foes, they scoff at them.
⁶ They think in their heart, "We shall
not be moved;
throughout all generations we shall
not meet adversity."

⁷ Their mouths are filled with cursing and
deceit and oppression;
under their tongues are mischief
and iniquity.
⁸ They sit in ambush in the villages;
in hiding places they murder the innocent.

Their eyes stealthily watch for the helpless;
⁹ they lurk in secret like a lion in its covert;
they lurk that they may seize the poor;
they seize the poor and drag them
off in their net.

¹⁰ They stoop, they crouch,
and the helpless fall by their might.
¹¹ They think in their heart, "God has forgotten,
he has hidden his face, he will never see it."

¹² Rise up, O Lord; O God, lift up your hand;
do not forget the oppressed.
¹³ Why do the wicked renounce God,
and say in their hearts, "You will not
call us to account"?

¹⁴ But you do see! Indeed you note
trouble and grief,
that you may take it into your hands;
the helpless commit themselves to you;
you have been the helper of the orphan.

¹⁵ Break the arm of the wicked and evildoers;
seek out their wickedness until
you find none.
¹⁶ The Lord is king forever and ever;
the nations shall perish from his land.

¹⁷ O Lord, you will hear the desire of the meek;
you will strengthen their heart,
you will incline your ear
¹⁸ to do justice for the orphan and the oppressed,
so that those from earth may strike
terror no more.

Meaning of Heb uncertain
Gk Syr Jerome Tg: Heb *flee
to your mountain, O bird*

IV Confidence
I Lament

Psalm 11

To the leader. Of David.

In the Lord I take refuge; how can
you say to me,
"Flee like a bird to the mountains;
² for look, the wicked bend the bow,
they have fitted their arrow to the string,
to shoot in the dark at the upright in heart.
³ If the foundations are destroyed,
what can the righteous do?"

⁴ The Lord is in his holy temple;
the Lord's throne is in heaven.
His eyes behold, his gaze examines
humankind.
⁵ The Lord tests the righteous and the wicked,
and his soul hates the lover of violence.
⁶ On the wicked he will rain coals
of fire and sulfur;
a scorching wind shall be the
portion of their cup.
⁷ For the Lord is righteous;
he loves righteous deeds;
the upright shall behold his face.

Psalm 12

To the leader: according to The Sheminith.
A Psalm of David.

Help, O Lord, for there is no longer
anyone who is godly;
the faithful have disappeared
from humankind.
² They utter lies to each other;
with flattering lips and a double
heart they speak.

³ May the Lord cut off all flattering lips,
the tongue that makes great boasts,
⁴ those who say, "With our tongues
we will prevail;
our lips are our own—who is our master?"

⁵ Because the poor are despoiled, because
the needy groan,
I will now rise up," says the Lord;
"I will place them in the safety for
which they long."
⁶ The promises of the Lord are promises
that are pure,
silver refined in a furnace on the ground,
purified seven times.

7 You, O LORD, will protect us;
    you will guard us from this
        generation forever.
8 On every side the wicked prowl,
    as vileness is exalted among humankind.

Psalm 13

To the leader. A Psalm of David.

How long, O LORD? Will you forget me forever?
    How long will you hide your face from me?
2 How long must I bear pain in my soul,
    and have sorrow in my heart all day long?
    How long shall my enemy be exalted over me?

3 Consider and answer me, O LORD my God!
    Give light to my eyes, or I will sleep the
        sleep of death,
4 and my enemy will say, "I have prevailed";
    my foes will rejoice because I am shaken.

5 But I trusted in your steadfast love;
    my heart shall rejoice in your salvation.
6 I will sing to the LORD,
    because he has dealt bountifully with me.

Psalm 14

To the leader. Of David.

Fools say in their hearts, "There is no God."
    They are corrupt, they do abominable deeds;
    there is no one who does good.

2 The LORD looks down from heaven
        on humankind
    to see if there are any who are wise,
    who seek after God.

3 They have all gone astray, they are all
        alike perverse;
    there is no one who does good,
    no, not one.

4 Have they no knowledge, all the evildoers
    who eat up my people as they eat bread,
    and do not call upon the LORD?

5 There they shall be in great terror,
    for God is with the company of the righteous.
6 You would confound the plans of the poor,
    but the LORD is their refuge.

7 O that deliverance for Israel would
        come from Zion!
    When the LORD restores the fortunes
        of his people,
    Jacob will rejoice; Israel will be glad.

Psalm 15

A Psalm of David.

O LORD, who may abide in your tent?
    Who may dwell on your holy hill?

2 Those who walk blamelessly, and do
        what is right,
    and speak the truth from their heart;
3 who do not slander with their tongue,
    and do no evil to their friends,
    nor take up a reproach against
        their neighbors;
4 in whose eyes the wicked are despised,
    but who honor those who fear the LORD;
    who stand by their oath even to their hurt;
5 who do not lend money at interest,
    and do not take a bribe against the innocent.

Those who do these things shall
    never be moved.

Psalm 16

A Miktam of David.

Protect me, O God, for in you I take refuge.
2 I say to the LORD, "You are my Lord;
    I have no good apart from you."

3 As for the holy ones in the land, they
        are the noble,
    in whom is all my delight.

4 Those who choose another god multiply
        their sorrows;
    their drink offerings of blood I will
        not pour out
    or take their names upon my lips.

5 The LORD is my chosen portion and my cup;
    you hold my lot.
6 The boundary lines have fallen for me
    in pleasant places;
    I have a goodly heritage.

k Syr: Heb hold counsels
l Jerome Tg: Meaning of
    Heb uncertain
m Cn: Meaning of Heb
    uncertain

I Lament
VI Liturgy
IV Confidence

7 I bless the LORD who gives me counsel;
    in the night also my heart instructs me.
8 I keep the LORD always before me;
    because he is at my right hand,
    I shall not be moved.

9 Therefore my heart is glad, and my
        soul rejoices;
    my body also rests secure.
10 For you do not give me up to Sheol,
    or let your faithful one see the Pit.

11 You show me the path of life.
    In your presence there is fullness of joy;
    in your right hand are pleasures
        forevermore.

Psalm 17

A Prayer of David.

Hear a just cause, O LORD; attend to my cry;
    give ear to my prayer from lips free of deceit.
2 From you let my vindication come;
    let your eyes see the right.

3 If you try my heart, if you visit me by night,
    if you test me, you will find no
        wickedness in me;
    my mouth does not transgress.
4 As for what others do, by the word of your lips
    I have avoided the ways of the violent.
5 My steps have held fast to your paths;
    my feet have not slipped.

6 I call upon you, for you will answer me, O God;
    incline your ear to me, hear my words.
7 Wondrously show your steadfast love,
    O savior of those who seek refuge
    from their adversaries at your right hand.

8 Guard me as the apple of the eye;
    hide me in the shadow of your wings,
9 from the wicked who despoil me,
    my deadly enemies who surround me.
10 They close their hearts to pity;
    with their mouths they speak arrogantly.
11 They track me down; now they surround me;
    they set their eyes to cast me to the ground.
12 They are like a lion eager to tear,
    like a young lion lurking in ambush.

ⁿ One Ms Compare Syr: MT
    our steps

I Lament
III Thanksgiving

13 Rise up, O LORD, confront them,
        overthrow them!

By your sword deliver my life
    from the wicked,
14 from mortals – by your hand, O LORD –
    from mortals whose portion in life is
        in this world.
May their bellies be filled with what you have
        stored up for them;
    may their children have more than enough;
    may they leave something over to
        their little ones.

15 As for me, I shall behold your face
    in righteousness;
    when I awake I shall be satisfied,
        beholding your likeness.

Psalm 18

To the leader. A Psalm of David the servant of
the LORD, who addressed the words of this
song to the LORD on the day when the LORD
delivered him from the hand of all his
enemies, and from the hand of Saul. He said:

I love you, O LORD, my strength.
2 The LORD is my rock, my fortress,
    and my deliverer,
    my God, my rock in whom I take refuge,
    my shield, and the horn of my salvation,
        my stronghold.
3 I call upon the LORD, who is worthy
    to be praised,
    so I shall be saved from my enemies.

4 The cords of death encompassed me;
    the torrents of perdition assailed me;
5 the cords of Sheol entangled me;
    the snares of death confronted me.

6 In my distress I called upon the LORD;
    to my God I cried for help.
    From his temple he heard my voice,
    and my cry to him reached his ears.

7 Then the earth reeled and rocked;
    the foundations also of the
        mountains trembled
    and quaked, because he was angry.
8 Smoke went up from his nostrils,
    and devouring fire from his mouth;
    glowing coals flamed forth from him.
9 He bowed the heavens, and came down;
    thick darkness was under his feet.
10 He rode on a cherub, and flew;
    he came swiftly upon the wings of the wind.

¹¹ He made darkness his covering around him,
    his canopy thick clouds dark with water.
¹² Out of the brightness before him
    there broke through his clouds
    hailstones and coals of fire.
¹³ The LORD also thundered in the heavens,
    and the Most High uttered his voice.
¹⁴ And he sent out his arrows,
        and scattered them;
    he flashed forth lightnings, and routed them.
¹⁵ Then the channels of the sea were seen,
    and the foundations of the world
        were laid bare
    at your rebuke, O LORD,
        at the blast of the breath of your nostrils.

¹⁶ He reached down from on high, he took me;
    he drew me out of mighty waters.
¹⁷ He delivered me from my strong enemy,
    and from those who hated me;
    for they were too mighty for me.
¹⁸ They confronted me in the day of my calamity;
    but the LORD was my support.
¹⁹ He brought me out into a broad place;
    he delivered me, because he delighted in me.

²⁰ The LORD rewarded me according
        to my righteousness;
    according to the cleanness of my hands he
        recompensed me.
²¹ For I have kept the ways of the LORD,
    and have not wickedly departed
        from my God.
²² For all his ordinances were before me,
    and his statutes I did not put away from me.
²³ I was blameless before him,
    and I kept myself from guilt.
²⁴ Therefore the LORD has recompensed me
        according to my righteousness,
    according to the cleanness of my
        hands in his sight.

²⁵ With the loyal you show yourself loyal;
    with the blameless you show
        yourself blameless;
²⁶ with the pure you show yourself pure;
    and with the crooked you show
        yourself perverse.
²⁷ For you deliver a humble people,
    but the haughty eyes you bring down.
²⁸ It is you who light my lamp;
    the LORD, my God, lights up my darkness.
²⁹ By you I can crush a troop,
    and by my God I can leap over a wall.

³⁰ This God—his way is perfect;
    the promise of the LORD proves true;
    he is a shield for all who take refuge in him.

³¹ For who is God except the LORD?
    And who is a rock besides our God?—
³² the God who girded me with strength,
    and made my way safe.
³³ He made my feet like the feet of a deer,
    and set me secure on the heights.
³⁴ He trains my hands for war,
    so that my arms can bend a bow of bronze.
³⁵ You have given me the shield of your salvation,
    and your right hand has supported me;
    your help has made me great.
³⁶ You gave me a wide place for my
        steps under me,
    and my feet did not slip.
³⁷ I pursued my enemies and overtook them;
    and did not turn back until they
        were consumed.
³⁸ I struck them down, so that they were
        not able to rise;
    they fell under my feet.
³⁹ For you girded me with strength for the battle;
    you made my assailants sink under me.
⁴⁰ You made my enemies turn their backs to me,
    and those who hated me I destroyed.
⁴¹ They cried for help, but there was no
        one to save them;
    they cried to the LORD, but he did
        not answer them.
⁴² I beat them fine, like dust before the wind;
    I cast them out like the mire of the streets.

⁴³ You delivered me from strife with the peoples;
    you made me head of the nations;
    people whom I had not known served me.
⁴⁴ As soon as they heard of me they obeyed me;
    foreigners came cringing to me.
⁴⁵ Foreigners lost heart,
    and came trembling out of their strongholds.

⁴⁶ The LORD lives! Blessed be my rock,
    and exalted be the God of my salvation,
⁴⁷ the God who gave me vengeance
    and subdued peoples under me;
⁴⁸ who delivered me from my enemies;
    indeed, you exalted me above
        my adversaries;
    you delivered me from the violent.

⁴⁹ For this I will extol you, O LORD,
        among the nations,

RSB
Psalm 18 v 25
Psalm 18 v 44

*Gk See 2 Sam 22.14; Heb
adds hailstones and
coals of fire
*Or gentleness
*Gk Tg: Heb people

and sing praises to your name.
50 Great triumphs he gives to his king,
    and shows steadfast love to his anointed,
    to David and his descendants forever.

Psalm 19

To the leader. A Psalm of David.

The heavens are telling the glory of God;
    and the firmament proclaims his handiwork.
2 Day to day pours forth speech,
    and night to night declares knowledge.
3 There is no speech, nor are there words;
    their voice is not heard;
4 yet their voice goes out through all the earth,
    and their words to the end of the world.

In the heavens he has set a tent for the sun,
5 which comes out like a bridegroom from
        his wedding canopy,
    and like a strong man runs its
        course with joy.
6 Its rising is from the end of the heavens,
    and its circuit to the end of them;
    and nothing is hid from its heat.

7 The law of the LORD is perfect,
    reviving the soul;
    the decrees of the LORD are sure,
    making wise the simple;
8 the precepts of the LORD are right,
    rejoicing the heart;
    the commandment of the LORD is clear,
    enlightening the eyes;
9 the fear of the LORD is pure,
    enduring forever;
    the ordinances of the LORD are true
    and righteous altogether.
10 More to be desired are they than gold,
    even much fine gold;
    sweeter also than honey,
    and drippings of the honeycomb.

11 Moreover by them is your servant warned;
    in keeping them there is great reward.
12 But who can detect their errors?
    Clear me from hidden faults.
13 Keep back your servant also from
        the insolent;
    do not let them have dominion over me.
    Then I shall be blameless,
    and innocent of great transgression.

* Or *dome*
s Gk Jerome Compare Syr:
  Heb *line*
t Heb *In them*
u Or *from proud thoughts*
v Gk: Heb *give victory,
  O LORD; let the King answer
  us when we call*

11 Hymn [Psalm 19 v.1–6]
v Wisdom [Psalm 19 v.7–14]
VII Royal

14 Let the words of my mouth and the
        meditation of my heart
    be acceptable to you,
    O LORD, my rock and my redeemer.

Psalm 20

To the leader. A Psalm of David.

The LORD answer you in the day of trouble!
    The name of the God of Jacob protect you!
2 May he send you help from the sanctuary,
    and give you support from Zion.
3 May he remember all your offerings,
    and regard with favor your
        burnt sacrifices.   Selah

4 May he grant you your heart's desire,
    and fulfill all your plans.
5 May we shout for joy over your victory,
    and in the name of our God set
        up our banners.
    May the LORD fulfill all your petitions.

6 Now I know that the LORD will
        help his anointed;
    he will answer him from his holy heaven
    with mighty victories by his right hand.
7 Some take pride in chariots,
        and some in horses,
    but our pride is in the name of the
        LORD our God.
8 They will collapse and fall,
    but we shall rise and stand upright.

9 Give victory to the king, O LORD,
    answer us when we call.

Psalm 21

To the leader: A Psalm of David.

In your strength the king rejoices, O LORD,
    and in your help how greatly he exults!
2 You have given him his heart's desire,
    and have not withheld the request
        of his lips.   Selah
3 For you meet him with rich blessings;
    you set a crown of fine gold on his head.
4 He asked you for life; you gave it to him—
    length of days forever and ever.
5 His glory is great through your help;
    splendor and majesty you bestow on him.
6 You bestow on him blessings forever;

you make him glad with the joy
    of your presence.
7 For the king trusts in the LORD,
    and through the steadfast love of the
      Most High he shall not be moved.

8 Your hand will find out all your enemies;
    your right hand will find out those
      who hate you.
9 You will make them like a fiery furnace
    when you appear.
The LORD will swallow them up in his wrath,
    and fire will consume them.
10 You will destroy their offspring from the earth,
    and their children from among humankind.
11 If they plan evil against you,
    if they devise mischief, they will not succeed.
12 For you will put them to flight;
    you will aim at their faces with your bows.

13 Be exalted, O LORD, in your strength!
    we will sing and praise your power.

Psalm 22

To the leader: according to The Deer of the Dawn.
A Psalm of David.

My God, my God, why have you forsaken me?
    Why are you so far from helping me, from the
      words of my groaning?
2 O my God, I cry by day, but you do not answer;
    and by night, but find no rest.

3 Yet you are holy,
    enthroned on the praises of Israel.
4 In you our ancestors trusted;
    they trusted, and you delivered them.
5 To you they cried, and were saved;
    in you they trusted, and were not
      put to shame.

6 But I am a worm, and not human;
    scorned by others, and despised
      by the people.
7 All who see me mock at me;
    they make mouths at me, they shake
      their heads;
8 "Commit your cause to the LORD;
    let him deliver—
    let him rescue the one in whom he delights!"

9 Yet it was you who took me from the womb;
    you kept me safe on my mother's breast.

10 On you I was cast from my birth,
    and since my mother bore me you have
      been my God.
11 Do not be far from me,
    for trouble is near
    and there is no one to help.

12 Many bulls encircle me,
    strong bulls of Bashan surround me;
13 they open wide their mouths at me,
    like a ravening and roaring lion.

14 I am poured out like water,
    and all my bones are out of joint;
my heart is like wax;
    it is melted within my breast;
15 my mouth is dried up like a potsherd,
    and my tongue sticks to my jaws;
    you lay me in the dust of death.

16 For dogs are all around me;
    a company of evildoers encircles me.
My hands and feet have shriveled;
17 I can count all my bones.
They stare and gloat over me;
18 they divide my clothes among themselves,
    and for my clothing they cast lots.

19 But you, O LORD, do not be far away!
    O my help, come quickly to my aid!
20 Deliver my soul from the sword,
    my life from the power of the dog!
21   Save me from the mouth of the lion!

From the horns of the wild oxen you
    have rescued me.
22 I will tell of your name to my brothers
    and sisters;
    in the midst of the congregation
    I will praise you:
23 You who fear the LORD, praise him!
All you offspring of Jacob, glorify him;
    stand in awe of him, all you
      offspring of Israel!
24 For he did not despise or abhor
    the affliction of the afflicted;
he did not hide his face from me,
    but heard when I cried to him.

25 From you comes my praise in the
    great congregation;
    my vows I will pay before those
      who fear him.
26 The poor shall eat and be satisfied;

RSB
Psalm 22:6

w Cn: Heb strength
x Meaning of Heb uncertain
y Heb my only one
z Heb answered
a Or kindred
b Heb him
c Heb he
d Or afflicted

1 Lament

those who seek him shall praise the LORD.
May your hearts live forever!

27 All the ends of the earth shall remember
and turn to the LORD;
and all the families of the nations
shall worship before him.
28 For dominion belongs to the LORD,
and he rules over the nations.

29 To him, indeed, shall all who sleep in
the earth bow down;
before him shall bow all who go
down to the dust,
and I shall live for him.
30 Posterity will serve him;
future generations will be told
about the Lord,
31 and proclaim his deliverance to a
people yet unborn,
saying that he has done it.

Psalm 23

A Psalm of David.

The LORD is my shepherd, I shall not want.
2   He makes me lie down in green pastures;
he leads me beside still waters;
3   he restores my soul.
He leads me in right paths
for his name's sake.

4 Even though I walk through
the darkest valley,
I fear no evil;
for you are with me;
your rod and your staff—
they comfort me.

5 You prepare a table before me
in the presence of my enemies;
you anoint my head with oil;
my cup overflows.
6 Surely goodness and mercy shall follow me
all the days of my life,
and I shall dwell in the house of the LORD
my whole life long.

e Gk Syr Jerome : Heb you
f Cn: Heb They have eaten
and
g Cn: Heb all the fat ones
h Compare Gk Syr Vg: Heb
and he who cannot keep
himself alive
i Compare Gk: Heb it will
be told about the Lord to
the generation; they
will come and
j Heb waters of rest
k Or life
l Or paths of righteousness
m Or the valley of the
shadow of death
n Or Only
o Or kindness
p Heb for length of days
q Gk Syr: Heb your face,
O Jacob

IV Confidence
VI Liturgy
I Lament

Psalm 24

Of David. A Psalm.

The earth is the LORD's and all that is in it,
the world, and those who live in it;
2 for he has founded it on the seas,
and established it on the rivers.

3 Who shall ascend the hill of the LORD?
And who shall stand in his holy place?
4 Those who have clean hands and pure hearts,
who do not lift up their souls to what is false,
and do not swear deceitfully.
5 They will receive blessing from the LORD,
and vindication from the God
of their salvation.
6 Such is the company of those who seek him,
who seek the face of the God of Jacob.   Selah

7 Lift up your heads, O gates!
and be lifted up, O ancient doors!
that the King of glory may come in.
8 Who is the King of glory?
The LORD, strong and mighty,
the LORD, mighty in battle.
9 Lift up your heads, O gates!
and be lifted up, O ancient doors!
that the King of glory may come in.
10 Who is this King of glory?
The LORD of hosts,
he is the King of glory.   Selah

Psalm 25

Of David.

To you, O LORD, I lift up my soul.
2 O my God, in you I trust;
do not let me be put to shame;
do not let my enemies exult over me.
3 Do not let those who wait for you
be put to shame;
let them be ashamed who are
wantonly treacherous.

4 Make me to know your ways, O LORD;
teach me your paths.
5 Lead me in your truth, and teach me,
for you are the God of my salvation;
for you I wait all day long.

6 Be mindful of your mercy, O LORD,
and of your steadfast love,
for they have been from of old.

⁷ Do not remember the sins of my youth
    or my transgressions;
  according to your steadfast love
    remember me,
  for your goodness' sake, O Lord!

⁸ Good and upright is the Lord;
  therefore he instructs sinners in the way.
⁹ He leads the humble in what is right,
  and teaches the humble his way.
¹⁰ All the paths of the Lord are steadfast
    love and faithfulness,
  for those who keep his covenant
    and his decrees.

¹¹ For your name's sake, O Lord,
  pardon my guilt, for it is great.
¹² Who are they that fear the Lord?
  He will teach them the way that
    they should choose.

¹³ They will abide in prosperity,
  and their children shall possess the land.
¹⁴ The friendship of the Lord is for
    those who fear him,
  and he makes his covenant known to them.
¹⁵ My eyes are ever toward the Lord,
  for he will pluck my feet out of the net.

¹⁶ Turn to me and be gracious to me,
  for I am lonely and afflicted.
¹⁷ Relieve the troubles of my heart,
  and bring me out of my distress.
¹⁸ Consider my affliction and my trouble,
  and forgive all my sins.

¹⁹ Consider how many are my foes,
  and with what violent hatred they hate me.
²⁰ O guard my life, and deliver me;
  do not let me be put to shame, for
    I take refuge in you.
²¹ May integrity and uprightness preserve me,
  for I wait for you.

²² Redeem Israel, O God,
  out of all its troubles.

Psalm 26

Of David.

Vindicate me, O Lord,
  for I have walked in my integrity,
  and I have trusted in the Lord

without wavering.
² Prove me, O Lord, and try me;
  test my heart and mind.
³ For your steadfast love is before my eyes,
  and I walk in faithfulness to you.

⁴ I do not sit with the worthless,
  nor do I consort with hypocrites;
⁵ I hate the company of evildoers,
  and will not sit with the wicked.

⁶ I wash my hands in innocence,
  and go around your altar, O Lord,
⁷ singing aloud a song of thanksgiving,
  and telling all your wondrous deeds.

⁸ O Lord, I love the house in which you dwell,
  and the place where your glory abides.
⁹ Do not sweep me away with sinners,
  nor my life with the bloodthirsty,
¹⁰ those in whose hands are evil devices,
  and whose right hands are full of bribes.

¹¹ But as for me, I walk in my integrity;
  redeem me, and be gracious to me.
¹² My foot stands on level ground;
  in the great congregation I will
    bless the Lord.

Psalm 27

Of David.

The Lord is my light and my salvation;
  whom shall I fear?
The Lord is the stronghold of my life;
  of whom shall I be afraid?

² When evildoers assail me
  to devour my flesh —
my adversaries and foes —
  they shall stumble and fall.

³ Though an army encamp against me,
  my heart shall not fear;
though war rise up against me,
  yet I will be confident.

⁴ One thing I asked of the Lord,
  that will I seek after:
to live in the house of the Lord
  all the days of my life,
to behold the beauty of the Lord,
  and to inquire in his temple.

ᵗ Or The troubles of
  my heart are enlarged;
  bring me
ᵘ Or in your faithfulness
ᵛ Or refuge

v.1 Liturgy
iv Confidence [Psalm 27 · v 1–6]
Lament [Psalm 27 · v 7–14]

5 For he will hide me in his shelter
    in the day of trouble;
he will conceal me under the cover of his tent;
    he will set me high on a rock.

6 Now my head is lifted up
    above my enemies all around me,
and I will offer in his tent
    sacrifices with shouts of joy;
I will sing and make melody to the Lord.

7 Hear, O Lord, when I cry aloud,
    be gracious to me and answer me!
8 "Come," my heart says, "seek his face!"
    Your face, Lord, do I seek.
9   Do not hide your face from me.

Do not turn your servant away in anger,
    you who have been my help.
Do not cast me off, do not forsake me,
    O God of my salvation!
10 If my father and mother forsake me,
    the Lord will take me up.

11 Teach me your way, O Lord,
    and lead me on a level path
    because of my enemies.
12 Do not give me up to the will of
    my adversaries,
    for false witnesses have risen against me,
    and they are breathing out violence.

13 I believe that I shall see the goodness
    of the Lord
    in the land of the living.
14 Wait for the Lord;
    be strong, and let your heart take courage;
    wait for the Lord!

Psalm 28

Of David.

To you, O Lord, I call;
    my rock, do not refuse to hear me,
for if you are silent to me,
    I shall be like those who go down to the Pit.
2 Hear the voice of my supplication,
    as I cry to you for help,
as I lift up my hands
    toward your most holy sanctuary.

3 Do not drag me away with the wicked,
    with those who are workers of evil,

who speak peace with their neighbors,
    while mischief is in their hearts.
4 Repay them according to their work,
    and according to the evil of their deeds;
repay them according to the work
    of their hands;
    render them their due reward.
5 Because they do not regard the works
    of the Lord,
    or the work of his hands,
he will break them down and build them
    up no more.

6 Blessed be the Lord,
    for he has heard the sound of my pleadings.
7 The Lord is my strength and my shield;
    in him my heart trusts;
so I am helped, and my heart exults,
    and with my song I give thanks to him.

8 The Lord is the strength of his people;
    he is the saving refuge of his anointed.
9 O save your people, and bless your heritage;
    be their shepherd, and carry them forever.

Psalm 29

A Psalm of David.

Ascribe to the Lord, O heavenly beings,
    ascribe to the Lord glory and strength.
2 Ascribe to the Lord the glory of his name;
    worship the Lord in holy splendor.

3 The voice of the Lord is over the waters;
    the God of glory thunders,
    the Lord, over mighty waters.
4 The voice of the Lord is powerful;
    the voice of the Lord is full of majesty.

5 The voice of the Lord breaks the cedars;
    the Lord breaks the cedars of Lebanon.
6 He makes Lebanon skip like a calf,
    and Sirion like a young wild ox.

7 The voice of the Lord flashes forth
    flames of fire.
8 The voice of the Lord shakes the wilderness;
    the Lord shakes the wilderness of Kadesh.

9 The voice of the Lord causes the
    oaks to whirl,
    and strips the forest bare;
    and in his temple all say, "Glory!"

10 The LORD sits enthroned over the flood;
  the LORD sits enthroned as king forever.
11 May the LORD give strength to his people!
  May the LORD bless his people with peace!

Psalm 30

A Psalm. A Song at the dedication of the temple.
Of David.

I will extol you, O LORD, for you have
    drawn me up,
  and did not let my foes rejoice over me.
2 O LORD my God, I cried to you for help,
  and you have healed me.
3 O LORD, you brought up my soul from Sheol,
  restored me to life from among those
    gone down to the Pit.

4 Sing praises to the LORD, O you his
    faithful ones,
  and give thanks to his holy name.
5 For his anger is but for a moment;
  his favor is for a lifetime.
  Weeping may linger for the night,
    but joy comes with the morning.

6 As for me, I said in my prosperity,
  "I shall never be moved."
7 By your favor, O LORD,
    you had established me as a
    strong mountain;
  you hid your face;
    I was dismayed.

8 To you, O LORD, I cried,
  and to the LORD I made supplication:
9 "What profit is there in my death,
    if I go down to the Pit?
  Will the dust praise you?
    Will it tell of your faithfulness?
10 Hear, O LORD, and be gracious to me!
  O LORD, be my helper!"

11 You have turned my mourning into dancing;
  you have taken off my sackcloth
    and clothed me with joy,
12 so that my soul may praise you and
    not be silent.
  O LORD my God, I will give thanks
    to you forever.

Psalm 31

To the leader. A Psalm of David.

In you, O LORD, I seek refuge;
  do not let me ever be put to shame;
  in your righteousness deliver me.
2 Incline your ear to me;
  rescue me speedily.
  Be a rock of refuge for me,
    a strong fortress to save me.

3 You are indeed my rock and my fortress;
  for your name's sake lead me and guide me,
4 take me out of the net that is hidden for me,
  for you are my refuge.
5 Into your hand I commit my spirit;
  you have redeemed me, O LORD, faithful God.

6 You hate those who pay regard to
    worthless idols,
  but I trust in the LORD.
7 I will exult and rejoice in your steadfast love,
  because you have seen my affliction;
  you have taken heed of my adversities,
8 and have not delivered me into the hand
    of the enemy;
  you have set my feet in a broad place.

9 Be gracious to me, O LORD, for I am in distress;
  my eye wastes away from grief,
  my soul and body also.
10 For my life is spent with sorrow,
  and my years with sighing;
  my strength fails because of my misery,
  and my bones waste away.

11 I am the scorn of all my adversaries,
  a horror to my neighbors,
  an object of dread to my acquaintances;
  those who see me in the street flee from me.
12 I have passed out of mind like one who is dead;
  I have become like a broken vessel.
13 For I hear the whispering of many—
    terror all around!—
  as they scheme together against me,
  as they plot to take my life.

14 But I trust in you, O LORD;
  I say, "You are my God."
15 My times are in your hand;
  deliver me from the hand of my
    enemies and persecutors.
16 Let your face shine upon your servant;
  save me in your steadfast love.

x Or that I should not go
   down to the Pit
y Heb that glory
z One Heb Ms Gk Syr
   Jerome: MT I hate
a Gk Syr: Heb my iniquity
b Cn: Heb exceedingly

111 Thanksgiving
1 Lament

17 Do not let me be put to shame, O LORD,
    for I call on you;
let the wicked be put to shame;
    let them go dumbfounded to Sheol.
18 Let the lying lips be stilled
    that speak insolently against the righteous
    with pride and contempt.

19 O how abundant is your goodness
    that you have laid up for those who fear you,
and accomplished for those who take
    refuge in you,
    in the sight of everyone!
20 In the shelter of your presence you hide them
    from human plots;
you hold them safe under your shelter
    from contentious tongues.

21 Blessed be the LORD,
    for he has wondrously shown his
    steadfast love to me
    when I was beset as a city under siege.
22 I had said in my alarm,
    "I am driven far from your sight."
But you heard my supplications
    when I cried out to you for help.

23 Love the LORD, all you his saints.
    The LORD preserves the faithful,
    but abundantly repays the one who
    acts haughtily.
Be strong, and let your heart take courage,
    all you who wait for the LORD.

Psalm 32

Of David. A Maskil.

**Happy are those whose transgression
is forgiven,
whose sin is covered.**

2 Happy are those to whom the LORD
    imputes no iniquity,
    and in whose spirit there is no deceit.

3 While I kept silence, my body wasted away
    through my groaning all day long.
4 For day and night your hand was
    heavy upon me;
    my strength was dried up as by the
    heat of summer.   Selah

c Another reading is cut off
d Meaning of Heb uncertain
e Cn: Heb at a time of
   finding only

III Thanksgiving
11 Hymn

5 Then I acknowledged my sin to you,
    and I did not hide my iniquity;
I said, "I will confess my transgressions
    to the LORD,"
    and you forgave the guilt of my sin.   Selah

6 Therefore let all who are faithful
    offer prayer to you;
at a time of distress, the rush of mighty waters
    shall not reach them.
7 You are a hiding place for me;
    you preserve me from trouble;
    you surround me with glad cries
    of deliverance.   Selah

8 I will instruct you and teach you the
    way you should go;
    I will counsel you with my eye upon you.
9 Do not be like a horse or a mule,
    without understanding,
    whose temper must be curbed with
    bit and bridle,
    else it will not stay near you.

10 Many are the torments of the wicked,
    but steadfast love surrounds those who
    trust in the LORD.
11 Be glad in the LORD and rejoice, O righteous,
    and shout for joy, all you upright in heart.

Psalm 33

Rejoice in the LORD, O you righteous.
    Praise befits the upright.
2 Praise the LORD with the lyre;
    make melody to him with the harp
    of ten strings.
3 Sing to him a new song;
    play skillfully on the strings,
    with loud shouts.

4 For the word of the LORD is upright,
    and all his work is done in faithfulness.
5 He loves righteousness and justice;
    the earth is full of the steadfast love
    of the LORD.

6 By the word of the LORD the heavens
    were made,
    and all their host by the breath of his mouth.
7 He gathered the waters of the sea as in a bottle;
    he put the deeps in storehouses.

8 Let all the earth fear the LORD;
　　let all the inhabitants of the world stand
　　　　in awe of him.
9 For he spoke, and it came to be;
　　he commanded, and it stood firm.

10 The LORD brings the counsel of the
　　　　nations to nothing;
　　he frustrates the plans of the peoples.
11 The counsel of the LORD stands forever,
　　the thoughts of his heart to all generations.
12 Happy is the nation whose God is the LORD,
　　the people whom he has chosen
　　　　as his heritage.

13 The LORD looks down from heaven;
　　he sees all humankind.
14 From where he sits enthroned he watches
　　all the inhabitants of the earth—
15 he who fashions the hearts of them all,
　　and observes all their deeds.
16 A king is not saved by his great army;
　　a warrior is not delivered by
　　　　his great strength.
17 The war horse is a vain hope for victory,
　　and by its great might it cannot save.

18 Truly the eye of the LORD is on those
　　　　who fear him,
　　on those who hope in his steadfast love,
19 to deliver their soul from death,
　　and to keep them alive in famine.

20 Our soul waits for the LORD;
　　he is our help and shield.
21 Our heart is glad in him,
　　because we trust in his holy name.
22 Let your steadfast love, O LORD, be upon us,
　　even as we hope in you.

Psalm 34

Of David, when he feigned madness before
Abimelech, so that he drove him out, and he went away.

1 I will bless the LORD at all times;
　　his praise shall continually be in my mouth.
2 My soul makes its boast in the LORD;
　　let the humble hear and be glad.
3 O magnify the LORD with me,
　　and let us exalt his name together.

4 I sought the LORD, and he answered me,
　　and delivered me from all my fears.

5 Look to him, and be radiant;
　　so your faces shall never be ashamed.
6 This poor soul cried, and was heard
　　　　by the LORD,
　　and was saved from every trouble.
7 The angel of the LORD encamps
　　around those who fear him,
　　and delivers them.
8 O taste and see that the LORD is good;
　　happy are those who take refuge in him.
9 O fear the LORD, you his holy ones,
　　for those who fear him have no want.
10 The young lions suffer want and hunger,
　　but those who seek the LORD
　　　　lack no good thing.

11 Come, O children, listen to me;
　　I will teach you the fear of the LORD.
12 Which of you desires life,
　　and covets many days to enjoy good?
13 Keep your tongue from evil,
　　and your lips from speaking deceit.
14 Depart from evil, and do good;
　　seek peace, and pursue it.

15 The eyes of the LORD are on the righteous,
　　and his ears are open to their cry.
16 The face of the LORD is against evildoers,
　　to cut off the remembrance of them
　　　　from the earth.
17 When the righteous cry for help,
　　the LORD hears,
　　and rescues them from all their troubles.
18 The LORD is near to the brokenhearted,
　　and saves the crushed in spirit.

19 Many are the afflictions of the righteous,
　　but the LORD rescues them from them all.
20 He keeps all their bones;
　　not one of them will be broken.
21 Evil brings death to the wicked,
　　and those who hate the righteous
　　　　will be condemned.
22 The LORD redeems the life of his servants;
　　none of those who take refuge in him
　　　　will be condemned.

Psalm 35

Of David.

Contend, O LORD, with those who
　　contend with me;
　　fight against those who fight against me!

RSB
Psalm 34:9-14

f Gk Syr Jerome: Heb their

III Thanksgiving
I Lament

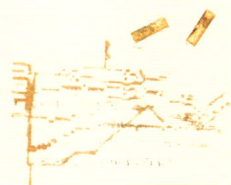

² Take hold of shield and buckler,
   and rise up to help me!
³ Draw the spear and javelin
   against my pursuers;
   say to my soul,
   "I am your salvation."

⁴ Let them be put to shame and dishonor
   who seek after my life.
   Let them be turned back and confounded
   who devise evil against me.
⁵ Let them be like chaff before the wind,
   with the angel of the LORD driving them on.
⁶ Let their way be dark and slippery,
   with the angel of the LORD pursuing them.

⁷ For without cause they hid their net for me;
   without cause they dug a pit for my life.
⁸ Let ruin come on them unawares.
   And let the net that they hid ensnare them;
   let them fall in it – to their ruin.

⁹ Then my soul shall rejoice in the LORD,
   exulting in his deliverance.
¹⁰ All my bones shall say,
   "O LORD, who is like you?
   You deliver the weak
   from those too strong for them,
   the weak and needy from those
   who despoil them."

¹¹ Malicious witnesses rise up;
   they ask me about things I do not know.
¹² They repay me evil for good;
   my soul is forlorn.
¹³ But as for me, when they were sick,
   I wore sackcloth;
   I afflicted myself with fasting.
   I prayed with head bowed on my bosom,
¹⁴   as though I grieved for a friend or a brother;
   I went about as one who laments for a mother,
   bowed down and in mourning.

RSB
Psalm 36:1

g Heb a pit, their net
h The word pit is
   transposed from the
   preceding line
i Or My prayer turned back
j Cn Compare Gk: Heb like
   the profanest of mockers
   of a cake
k Heb him

l Lament

¹⁵ But at my stumbling they gathered in glee,
   they gathered together against me;
   ruffians whom I did not know
   tore at me without ceasing;
¹⁶ they impiously mocked more and more,
   gnashing at me with their teeth.

¹⁷ How long, O LORD, will you look on?
   Rescue me from their ravages,
   my life from the lions!
¹⁸ Then I will thank you in the great congregation;

in the mighty throng I will praise you.

¹⁹ Do not let my treacherous enemies
   rejoice over me,
   or those who hate me without cause
   wink the eye.
²⁰ For they do not speak peace,
   but they conceive deceitful words
   against those who are quiet in the land.
²¹ They open wide their mouths against me;
   they say, "Aha, Aha,
   our eyes have seen it."

²² You have seen, O LORD; do not be silent!
   O LORD, do not be far from me!
²³ Wake up! Bestir yourself for my defense,
   for my cause, my God and my Lord!
²⁴ Vindicate me, O LORD, my God,
   according to your righteousness,
   and do not let them rejoice over me.
²⁵ Do not let them say to themselves,
   "Aha, we have our heart's desire."
   Do not let them say, "We have
   swallowed you up."

²⁶ Let all those who rejoice at my calamity
   be put to shame and confusion;
   let those who exalt themselves against me
   be clothed with shame and dishonor.

²⁷ Let those who desire my vindication
   shout for joy and be glad,
   and say evermore,
   "Great is the LORD,
   who delights in the welfare of his servant."
²⁸ Then my tongue shall tell of your
   righteousness
   and of your praise all day long.

Psalm 36

To the leader. Of David, the servant of the LORD.

¹ Transgression speaks to the wicked
   deep in their hearts;
   there is no fear of God
   before their eyes.
² For they flatter themselves in their own eyes
   that their iniquity cannot be found
   out and hated.
³ The words of their mouths are
   mischief and deceit;
   they have ceased to act wisely and do good.

4 They plot mischief while on their beds;
  they are set on a way that is not good;
  they do not reject evil.

5 Your steadfast love, O LORD, extends
    to the heavens,
  your faithfulness to the clouds.
6 Your righteousness is like the
    mighty mountains,
  your judgments are like the great deep;
  you save humans and animals alike, O LORD.

7 How precious is your steadfast love, O God!
  All people may take refuge in the
    shadow of your wings.
8 They feast on the abundance of your house,
  and you give them drink from the
    river of your delights.
9 For with you is the fountain of life;
  in your light we see light.

10 O continue your steadfast love to those
    who know you,
  and your salvation to the upright of heart!
11 Do not let the foot of the arrogant
    tread on me,
  or the hand of the wicked drive me away.
12 There the evildoers lie prostrate;
  they are thrust down, unable to rise.

Psalm 37

Of David.

Do not fret because of the wicked;
  do not be envious of wrongdoers,
2 for they will soon fade like the grass,
  and wither like the green herb.

3 Trust in the LORD, and do good;
  so you will live in the land,
    and enjoy security.
4 Take delight in the LORD,
  and he will give you the desires
    of your heart.

5 Commit your way to the LORD;
  trust in him, and he will act.
6 He will make your vindication shine
    like the light,
  and the justice of your cause
    like the noonday.

7 Be still before the LORD, and wait
    patiently for him;
  do not fret over those who prosper
    in their way,
  over those who carry out evil devices.

8 Refrain from anger, and forsake wrath.
  Do not fret—it leads only to evil.
9 For the wicked shall be cut off,
  but those who wait for the LORD
    shall inherit the land.

10 Yet a little while, and the wicked
    will be no more;
  though you look diligently for their place,
    they will not be there.
11 But the meek shall inherit the land,
  and delight themselves in
    abundant prosperity.

12 The wicked plot against the righteous,
  and gnash their teeth at them;
13 but the LORD laughs at the wicked,
  for he sees that their day is coming.

14 The wicked draw the sword and
    bend their bows
  to bring down the poor and needy,
  to kill those who walk uprightly;
15 their sword shall enter their own heart,
  and their bows shall be broken.

16 Better is a little that the righteous person has
  than the abundance of many wicked.
17 For the arms of the wicked shall be broken,
  but the LORD upholds the righteous.

18 The LORD knows the days of the blameless,
  and their heritage will abide forever;
19 they are not put to shame in evil times,
  in the days of famine they have abundance.

20 But the wicked perish,
  and the enemies of the LORD are like the
    glory of the pastures;
  they vanish—like smoke they vanish away.

21 The wicked borrow, and do not pay back,
  but the righteous are generous
    and keep giving;
22 for those blessed by the LORD shall
    inherit the land,
  but those cursed by him shall be cut off.

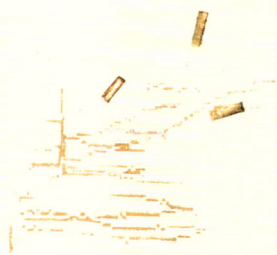

v. Wisdom

23 Our steps are made firm by the LORD,
   when he delights in our way;
24 though we stumble, we shall not
      fall headlong,
   for the LORD holds us by the hand.

25 I have been young, and now am old,
   yet I have not seen the righteous forsaken
   or their children begging bread.
26 They are ever giving liberally and lending,
   and their children become a blessing.

27 Depart from evil and do good;
   so you shall abide forever.
28 For the LORD loves justice;
   he will not forsake his faithful ones.

   The righteous shall be kept safe forever,
   but the children of the wicked
      shall be cut off.
29 The righteous shall inherit the land,
   and live in it forever.

30 The mouths of the righteous utter wisdom,
   and their tongues speak justice.
31 The law of their God is in their hearts;
   their steps do not slip.

32 The wicked watch for the righteous,
   and seek to kill them.
33 The LORD will not abandon them
      to their power,
   or let them be condemned when they
      are brought to trial.

34 Wait for the LORD, and keep to his way,
   and he will exalt you to inherit the land;
   you will look on the destruction
      of the wicked.

35 I have seen the wicked oppressing,
   and towering like a cedar of Lebanon.
36 Again I passed by, and they were no more;
   though I sought them, they could
      not be found.

37 Mark the blameless, and behold the upright,
   for there is posterity for the peaceable.
38 But transgressors shall be
      altogether destroyed;
   the posterity of the wicked shall be cut off.

39 The salvation of the righteous is
      from the LORD;

RSB
Psalm 38:6
Psalm 38:9

l Heb. A man's steps
m Heb. his
n Heb. he stumbles
o Heb. he!
p Heb. him
q Gk. Meaning of Heb.
      uncertain
r Gk. Syr. Jerome: Heb. he

1 Lament

he is their refuge in the time of trouble.
40 The LORD helps them and rescues them;
   he rescues them from the wicked,
      and saves them,
   because they take refuge in him.

Psalm 38

A Psalm of David, for the memorial offering.

O LORD, do not rebuke me
in your anger,
or discipline me in your wrath.

2 For your arrows have sunk into me,
   and your hand has come down on me.

3 There is no soundness in my flesh
   because of your indignation;
   there is no health in my bones
   because of my sin.
4 For my iniquities have gone over my head;
   they weigh like a burden too heavy for me.

5 My wounds grow foul and fester
   because of my foolishness;
6 I am utterly bowed down and prostrate;
   all day long I go around mourning.
7 For my loins are filled with burning,
   and there is no soundness in my flesh.
8 I am utterly spent and crushed;
   I groan because of the tumult of my heart.

9 O LORD, all my longing is known to you;
   my sighing is not hidden from you.
10 My heart throbs, my strength fails me;
   as for the light of my eyes—it also
      has gone from me.
11 My friends and companions stand aloof
      from my affliction,
   and my neighbors stand far off.

12 Those who seek my life lay their snares;
   those who seek to hurt me speak of ruin,
   and meditate treachery all day long.

13 But I am like the deaf, I do not hear;
   like the mute, who cannot speak.
14 Truly, I am like one who does not hear,
   and in whose mouth is no retort.

¹⁵ But it is for you, O LORD, that I wait;
it is you, O Lord my God, who will answer.
¹⁶ For I pray, "Only do not let them
rejoice over me,
those who boast against me when
my foot slips."

¹⁷ For I am ready to fall,
and my pain is ever with me.
¹⁸ I confess my iniquity;
I am sorry for my sin.
¹⁹ Those who are my foes without
cause are mighty,
and many are those who hate me wrongfully.
²⁰ Those who render me evil for good
are my adversaries because I
follow after good.

²¹ Do not forsake me, O LORD;
O my God, do not be far from me;
²² make haste to help me,
O Lord, my salvation.

Psalm 39

To the leader: to Jeduthun. A Psalm of David.

¹ I said, "I will guard my ways
that I may not sin with my tongue;
I will keep a muzzle on my mouth
as long as the wicked are in my presence."
² I was silent and still;
I held my peace to no avail;
my distress grew worse,
³ my heart became hot within me.
While I mused, the fire burned;
then I spoke with my tongue:

⁴ "LORD, let me know my end,
and what is the measure of my days;
let me know how fleeting my life is.
⁵ You have made my days a few handbreadths,
and my lifetime is as nothing in your sight.
Surely everyone stands as a mere breath. *Selah*
⁶ Surely everyone goes about like a shadow.
Surely for nothing they are in turmoil;
they heap up, and do not know
who will gather.

⁷ "And now, O Lord, what do I wait for?
My hope is in you.
⁸ Deliver me from all my transgressions.
Do not make me the scorn of the fool.
⁹ I am silent; I do not open my mouth,

for it is you who have done it.
¹⁰ Remove your stroke from me;
I am worn down by the blows of your hand.

¹¹ "You chastise mortals
in punishment for sin,
consuming like a moth what is dear to them;
surely everyone is a mere breath. *Selah*

¹² "Hear my prayer, O LORD,
and give ear to my cry;
do not hold your peace at my tears.
For I am your passing guest,
an alien, like all my forebears.
¹³ Turn your gaze away from me,
that I may smile again,
before I depart and am no more."

Psalm 40

To the leader. Of David. A Psalm.

¹ I waited patiently for the LORD;
he inclined to me and heard my cry.
² He drew me up from the desolate pit,
out of the miry bog,
and set my feet upon a rock,
making my steps secure.
³ He put a new song in my mouth,
a song of praise to our God.
Many will see and fear,
and put their trust in the LORD.

⁴ Happy are those who make
the LORD their trust,
who do not turn to the proud,
to those who go astray after false gods.
⁵ You have multiplied, O LORD my God,
your wondrous deeds and your
thoughts toward us;
none can compare with you.
Were I to proclaim and tell of them,
they would be more than can be counted.

⁶ Sacrifice and offering you do not desire,
but you have given me an open ear.
Burnt offering and sin offering
you have not required.
⁷ Then I said, "Here I am;
in the scroll of the book it is written of me.
⁸ I delight to do your will, O my God;
your law is within my heart."

RSB
Psalm 39:1-2

* QMs: MT *my living foes*
† *Heb* hostility
u *Cn: Heb* pit of tumult
v *Heb* ears you have dug
for me
w *Meaning of Heb
uncertain*

III Thanksgiving [Psalm 40 v 1-12]
I Lament [Psalm 40 v 13-17]

9 I have told the glad news of deliverance
   in the great congregation;
   see, I have not restrained my lips,
   as you know, O LORD.
10 I have not hidden your saving help
   within my heart,
   I have spoken of your faithfulness
   and your salvation;
   I have not concealed your steadfast love
   and your faithfulness
   from the great congregation.

11 Do not, O LORD, withhold
   your mercy from me;
   let your steadfast love and your faithfulness
   keep me safe forever.
12 For evils have encompassed me
   without number;
   my iniquities have overtaken me,
   until I cannot see;
   they are more than the hairs of my head,
   and my heart fails me.

13 Be pleased, O LORD, to deliver me;
   O LORD, make haste to help me.
14 Let all those be put to shame and confusion
   who seek to snatch away my life;
   let those be turned back and
   brought to dishonor
   who desire my hurt.
15 Let those be appalled because of their shame
   who say to me, "Aha, Aha!"

16 But may all who seek you
   rejoice and be glad in you;
   may those who love your salvation
   say continually, "Great is the LORD!"
17 As for me, I am poor and needy,
   but the Lord takes thought for me.
   You are my help and my deliverer;
   do not delay, O my God.

Psalm 41

To the leader. A Psalm of David.

Happy are those who consider the poor;
   the LORD delivers them in the day of trouble.
2 The LORD protects them and keeps them alive;
   they are called happy in the land.
   You do not give them up to the will
   of their enemies.
3 The LORD sustains them on their sickbed;
   in their illness you heal all their infirmities.

4 As for me, I said, "O LORD, be gracious to me;
   heal me, for I have sinned against you."
5 My enemies wonder in malice
   when I will die, and my name perish.
6 And when they come to see me,
   they utter empty words,
   while their hearts gather mischief;
   when they go out, they tell it abroad.
7 All who hate me whisper together about me;
   they imagine the worst for me.

8 They think that a deadly thing has
   fastened on me,
   that I will not rise again from where I lie.
9 Even my bosom friend in whom I trusted,
   who ate of my bread, has lifted the
   heel against me.
10 But you, O LORD, be gracious to me,
   and raise me up, that I may repay them.

11 By this I know that you are pleased with me;
   because my enemy has not
   triumphed over me.
12 But you have upheld me because
   of my integrity,
   and set me in your presence forever.

13 Blessed be the LORD, the God of Israel,
   from everlasting to everlasting.
   AMEN & AMEN

RSB
Psalm 40:10

x Or weak
y Heb you change all
   his bed

111 Thanksgiving

Psalm 42

BOOK II

To the leader. A Maskil of the Korahites.

¹ As a deer longs for flowing streams,
   so my soul longs for you, O God.
² My soul thirsts for God,
   for the living God.
   When shall I come and behold
   the face of God?
³ My tears have been my food
   day and night,
   while people say to me continually,
   "Where is your God?"

⁴ These things I remember,
   as I pour out my soul:
   how I went with the throng,
   and led them in procession to
      the house of God,
   with glad shouts and songs of thanksgiving,
   a multitude keeping festival.
⁵ Why are you cast down, O my soul,
   and why are you disquieted within me?
   Hope in God; for I shall again praise him,
   my help ⁶and my God.

My soul is cast down within me;
   therefore I remember you
   from the land of Jordan and of Hermon,
   from Mount Mizar.
⁷ Deep calls to deep
   at the thunder of your cataracts;
   all your waves and your billows
   have gone over me.
⁸ By day the LORD commands his steadfast love,
   and at night his song is with me,
   a prayer to the God of my life.

⁹ I say to God, my rock,
   "Why have you forgotten me?
   Why must I walk about mournfully
   because the enemy oppresses me?"
¹⁰ As with a deadly wound in my body,
   my adversaries taunt me,
   while they say to me continually,
   "Where is your God?"

¹¹ Why are you cast down, O my soul,
   and why are you disquieted within me?
   Hope in God; for I shall again praise him,
   my help and my God.

ᶻ Meaning of Heb uncertain

1 Lament

Psalm 43

Vindicate me, O God, and defend my cause
 against an ungodly people;
from those who are deceitful and unjust
 deliver me!
2 For you are the God in whom I take refuge;
 why have you cast me off?
Why must I walk about mournfully
 because of the oppression of the enemy?

3 O send out your light and your truth;
 let them lead me;
let them bring me to your holy hill
 and to your dwelling.
4 Then I will go to the altar of God,
 to God my exceeding joy;
and I will praise you with the harp,
 O God, my God.

5 Why are you cast down, O my soul,
 and why are you disquieted within me?
Hope in God; for I shall again praise him,
 my help and my God.

Psalm 44

To the leader. Of the Korahites. A Maskil.

We have heard with our ears, O God,
 our ancestors have told us,
what deeds you performed in their days,
 in the days of old:
2 you with your own hand drove out the nations,
 but them you planted;
you afflicted the peoples,
 but them you set free;
3 for not by their own sword did
 they win the land,
nor did their own arm give them victory;
but your right hand, and your arm,
 and the light of your countenance,
 for you delighted in them.

4 You are my King and my God;
 you command victories for Jacob.
5 Through you we push down our foes;
 through your name we tread
 down our assailants.
6 For not in my bow do I trust,
 nor can my sword save me.
7 But you have saved us from our foes,
 and have put to confusion those who hate us.

a Gk Syr: Heb *You are my
King, O God; command*
b Heb *a shaking of the head*

c Lament

8 In God we have boasted continually,
 and we will give thanks to
  your name forever. Selah

9 Yet you have rejected us and abased us,
 and have not gone out with our armies.
10 You made us turn back from the foe,
 and our enemies have gotten spoil.
11 You have made us like sheep for slaughter,
 and have scattered us among the nations.
12 You have sold your people for a trifle,
 demanding no high price for them.

13 You have made us the taunt of our neighbors,
 the derision and scorn of those around us.
14 You have made us a byword among the nations,
 a laughingstock among the peoples.
15 All day long my disgrace is before me,
 and shame has covered my face
16 at the words of the taunters and revilers,
 at the sight of the enemy and the avenger.

17 All this has come upon us,
 yet we have not forgotten you,
 or been false to your covenant.
18 Our heart has not turned back,
 nor have our steps departed from your way,
19 yet you have broken us in the haunt of jackals,
 and covered us with deep darkness.

20 If we had forgotten the name of our God,
 or spread out our hands to a strange god,
21 would not God discover this?
 For he knows the secrets of the heart.
22 Because of you we are being killed all day long,
 and accounted as sheep for the slaughter.

23 Rouse yourself! Why do you sleep, O Lord?
 Awake, do not cast us off forever!
24 Why do you hide your face?
 Why do you forget our affliction
 and oppression?
25 For we sink down to the dust;
 our bodies cling to the ground.
26 Rise up, come to our help.
 Redeem us for the sake of your
 steadfast love.

Psalm 45

To the leader: according to Lilies. Of the
Korahites. A Maskil. A love song.

My heart overflows with goodly theme;
   I address my verses to the king;
     my tongue is like the pen of a ready scribe.

2 You are the most handsome of men;
   grace is poured upon your lips;
     therefore God has blessed you forever.
3 Gird your sword on your thigh, O mighty one,
   in your glory and majesty.

4 In your majesty ride on victoriously
   for the cause of truth and to
     defend the right;
   let your right hand teach you dread deeds.
5 Your arrows are sharp
   in the heart of the king's enemies;
     the peoples fall under you.

6 Your throne, O God, endures forever and ever.
   Your royal scepter is a scepter of equity;
7 you love righteousness and hate wickedness.
   Therefore God, your God, has anointed you
     with the oil of gladness beyond
       your companions;
8 your robes are all fragrant with myrrh
   and aloes and cassia.
From ivory palaces stringed instruments
   make you glad;
9 daughters of kings are among your
     ladies of honor;
   at your right hand stands the queen in
     gold of Ophir.

10 Hear, O daughter, consider and
     incline your ear;
   forget your people and your father's house,
11 and the king will desire your beauty.
   Since he is your lord, bow to him;
12 the people of Tyre will seek your
     favor with gifts,
   the richest of the people 13 with all
     kinds of wealth.

The princess is decked in her chamber with
     gold-woven robes;
14 in many-colored robes she is led to the king;
   behind her the virgins, her
     companions, follow.
15 With joy and gladness they are led along
   as they enter the palace of the king.

16 In the place of ancestors you, O king,
     shall have sons;
   you will make them princes in all the earth.
17 I will cause your name to be celebrated
     in all generations;
   therefore the peoples will praise you
     forever and ever.

Psalm 46

To the leader. Of the Korahites.
According to Alamoth. A Song.

God is our refuge and strength,
   a very present help in trouble.
2 Therefore we will not fear, though the
     earth should change,
   though the mountains shake in the
     heart of the sea;
3 though its waters roar and foam,
   though the mountains tremble
     with its tumult.   Selah

4 There is a river whose streams make glad
     the city of God,
   the holy habitation of the Most High.
5 God is in the midst of the city;
   it shall not be moved;
   God will help it when the morning dawns.
6 The nations are in an uproar,
   the kingdoms totter;
   he utters his voice, the earth melts.
7 The LORD of hosts is with us;
   the God of Jacob is our refuge.   Selah

8 Come, behold the works of the LORD;
   see what desolations he has
     brought on the earth.
9 He makes wars cease to the end of the earth;
   he breaks the bow, and shatters the spear;
   he burns the shields with fire.
10 "Be still, and know that I am God!
   I am exalted among the nations,
   I am exalted in the earth."
11 The LORD of hosts is with us;
   the God of Jacob is our refuge.   Selah

Psalm 47

To the leader. Of the Korahites. A Psalm.

Clap your hands, all you peoples;
   shout to God with loud songs of joy.
2 For the LORD, the Most High, is awesome,

c Cn: Heb and the meekness of
d Or your throne is a
  throne of God. It
e Heb daughter
f Or people. 13 All glorious is
  the princess within; gold
  embroidery is her clothing
g Heb lacks O king
h Or well proved
i Heb of it
j,k Or fortress

VII Reval
VIII Zion songs
11 Hymn

a great king over all the earth.
³ He subdued peoples under us,
and nations under our feet.
⁴ He chose our heritage for us,
the pride of Jacob whom he loves.   *Selah*

⁵ God has gone up with a shout,
the LORD with the sound of a trumpet.
⁶ Sing praises to God, sing praises;
sing praises to our King, sing praises.
⁷ For God is the king of all the earth;
sing praises with a psalm.

⁸ God is king over the nations;
God sits on his holy throne.
⁹ The princes of the peoples gather
as the people of the God of Abraham.
For the shields of the earth belong to God;
he is highly exalted.

VIII
Psalm 48

A Song. A Psalm of the Korahites.

Great is the LORD and greatly to be praised
in the city of our God.
His holy mountain, beautiful in elevation,
is the joy of all the earth,
Mount Zion, in the far north,
the city of the great King.
³ Within its citadels God
has shown himself a sure defense.

⁴ Then the kings assembled,
they came on together.
⁵ As soon as they saw it, they were astounded;
they were in panic, they took to flight;
⁶ trembling took hold of them there,
pains as of a woman in labor,
⁷ as when an east wind shatters
the ships of Tarshish.
⁸ As we have heard, so have we seen
in the city of the LORD of hosts,
in the city of our God,
which God establishes forever.   *Selah*

⁹ We ponder your steadfast love, O God,
in the midst of your temple.
¹⁰ Your name, O God, like your praise,
reaches to the ends of the earth.
Your right hand is filled with victory.
¹¹ Let Mount Zion be glad,

RSV
Psalm 47:7
Psalm 48:9

l Heb *Maskil*
m Heb *daughters*
n *Another reading is* no one
can ransom a brother
o Heb *the pit*
p Gk Syr Compare Tg: Heb
their inward [*thought*]
q Tg: Heb *after them*
r Cn: Heb *the upright shall*
have dominion over them
in the morning

VIII Zion Songs
v Wisdom

let the towns of Judah rejoice
because of your judgments.

¹² Walk about Zion, go all around it,
count its towers,
¹³ consider well its ramparts;
go through its citadels,
that you may tell the next generation
¹⁴ that this is God,
our God forever and ever.
He will be our guide forever.

v
Psalm 49

To the leader. Of the Korahites. A Psalm.

Hear this, all you peoples;
give ear, all inhabitants of the world,
² both low and high,
rich and poor together.
³ My mouth shall speak wisdom;
the meditation of my heart shall be
understanding.
⁴ I will incline my ear to a proverb;
I will solve my riddle to the music
of the harp.

⁵ Why should I fear in times of trouble,
when the iniquity of my persecutors
surrounds me,
⁶ those who trust in their wealth
and boast of the abundance of their riches?
⁷ Truly, no ransom avails for one's life,
there is no price one can give to God for it.
⁸ For the ransom of life is costly,
and can never suffice,
⁹ that one should live on forever
and never see the grave.

¹⁰ When we look at the wise, they die;
fool and dolt perish together
and leave their wealth to others.
¹¹ Their graves are their homes forever,
their dwelling places to all generations,
though they named lands their own.
¹² Mortals cannot abide in their pomp;
they are like the animals that perish.

¹³ Such is the fate of the foolhardy,
the end of those who are pleased
with their lot.   *Selah*
¹⁴ Like sheep they are appointed for Sheol;
Death shall be their shepherd;
straight to the grave they descend,

and their form shall waste away;
   Sheol shall be their home.
[15] But God will ransom my soul from the
     power of Sheol,
   for he will receive me.   Selah

[16] Do not be afraid when some become rich,
   when the wealth of their houses increases,
[17] For when they die they will carry
     nothing away;
   their wealth will not go down after them.
[18] Though in their lifetime they count
     themselves happy
   —for you are praised when you do
     well for yourself—
[19] they will go to the company of their ancestors,
   who will never again see the light.
[20] Mortals cannot abide in their pomp;
   they are like the animals that perish.

Psalm 50

A Psalm of Asaph.

The mighty one, God the LORD,
   speaks and summons the earth
   from the rising of the sun to its setting.
[2] Out of Zion, the perfection of beauty,
   God shines forth.

[3] Our God comes and does not keep silence,
   before him is a devouring fire,
   and a mighty tempest all around him.
[4] He calls to the heavens above
   and to the earth, that he may
     judge his people:
[5] "Gather to me my faithful ones,
   who made a covenant with me by sacrifice!"
[6] The heavens declare his righteousness,
   for God himself is judge.   Selah

[7] Hear, O my people, and I will speak,
   O Israel, I will testify against you.
   I am God, your God.
[8] Not for your sacrifices do I rebuke you;
   your burnt offerings are continually
     before me.
[9] I will not accept a bull from your house,
   or goats from your folds.
[10] For every wild animal of the forest is mine,
   the cattle on a thousand hills.
[11] I know all the birds of the air,
   and all that moves in the field is mine.

[12] "If I were hungry, I would not tell you,
   for the world and all that is in it is mine.
[13] Do I eat the flesh of bulls,
   or drink the blood of goats?
[14] Offer to God a sacrifice of thanksgiving,
   and pay your vows to the Most High.
[15] Call on me in the day of trouble;
   I will deliver you, and you shall glorify me."

[16] But to the wicked God says:
   "What right have you to recite my statutes,
   or take my covenant on your lips?
[17] For you hate discipline,
   and you cast my words behind you.
[18] You make friends with a thief
     when you see one,
   and you keep company with adulterers.

[19] You give your mouth free rein for evil,
   and your tongue frames deceit.
[20] You sit and speak against your kin;
   you slander your own mother's child.
[21] These things you have done and I
     have been silent;
   you thought that I was one just like yourself.
   But now I rebuke you, and lay
     the charge before you.

[22] Mark this, then, you who forget God,
   or I will tear you apart, and there will be
     no one to deliver.
[23] Those who bring thanksgiving as their
     sacrifice honor me;
   to those who go the right way
   I will show the salvation of God."

Psalm 51

To the leader. A Psalm of David, when the
prophet Nathan came to him, after he had gone
in to Bathsheba.

Have mercy on me, O God,
according to your steadfast love;
according to your abundant mercy
blot out my transgressions.

[2] Wash me thoroughly from my iniquity,
   and cleanse me from my sin.

[3] For I know my transgressions,

[s] Meaning of Heb uncertain
[t] Cn: Heb you
[u] Gk Syr Tg: Heb mountains
[v] Or make thanksgiving your sacrifice to god
[w] Heb who set a way

VI Liturgy
I Lament

and my sin is ever before me.
4 Against you, you alone, have I sinned,
    and done what is evil in your sight,
so that you are justified in your sentence
    and blameless when you pass judgment.
5 Indeed, I was born guilty,
    a sinner when my mother conceived me.

6 You desire truth in the inward being;
    therefore teach me wisdom in
        my secret heart.
7 Purge me with hyssop, and I shall be clean;
    wash me, and I shall be whiter than snow.
8 Let me hear joy and gladness;
    let the bones that you have crushed rejoice.
9 Hide your face from my sins,
    and blot out all my iniquities.

10 Create in me a clean heart, O God,
    and put a new and right spirit within me.
11 Do not cast me away from your presence,
    and do not take your holy spirit from me.
12 Restore to me the joy of your salvation,
    and sustain in me a willing spirit.

13 Then I will teach transgressors your ways,
    and sinners will return to you.
14 Deliver me from bloodshed, O God,
    O God of my salvation,
    and my tongue will sing aloud of
        your deliverance.

15 O Lord, open my lips,
    and my mouth will declare your praise.
16 For you have no delight in sacrifice;
    if I were to give a burnt offering,
        you would not be pleased.
17 The sacrifice acceptable to God
    is a broken spirit;
a broken and contrite heart, O God,
    you will not despise.

18 Do good to Zion in your good pleasure;
    rebuild the walls of Jerusalem,
19 then you will delight in right sacrifices,
    in burnt offerings and whole burnt offerings;
    then bulls will be offered on your altar.

RSB
Psalm 51:15

a Meaning of Heb uncertain
b Or steadfast
c Or grievous
d Or My sacrifice, O God,
e Cn Compare Syr: Heb the
    kindness of God
f Heb him
g Syr Tg: Heb in his
    destruction
h Cn: Heb wait for

1 Lament

Psalm 52

To the leader. A Maskil of David, when Doeg the
Edomite came to Saul and said to him,
"David has come to the house of Ahimelech."

1 Why do you boast, O mighty one,
    of mischief done against the godly?
    All day long you are plotting destruction.
Your tongue is like a sharp razor,
    you worker of treachery.
3 You love evil more than good,
    and lying more than speaking
        the truth.   Selah
4 You love all words that devour,
    O deceitful tongue.

5 But God will break you down forever;
    he will snatch and tear you from your tent;
    he will uproot you from the land
        of the living.   Selah
6 The righteous will see, and fear,
    and will laugh at the evildoer, saying,
7 "See the one who would not take
        refuge in God,
    but trusted in abundant riches,
    and sought refuge in wealth!"

8 But I am like a green olive tree
    in the house of God.
I trust in the steadfast love of God
    forever and ever.
9 I will thank you forever,
    because of what you have done.
In the presence of the faithful
    I will proclaim your name, for it is good.

Psalm 53

To the leader: according to Mahalath. A Maskil of David.

1 Fools say in their hearts, "There is no God."
    They are corrupt, they commit
        abominable acts;
    there is no one who does good.

2 God looks down from heaven on humankind
    to see if there are any who are wise,
    who seek after God.

3 They have all fallen away, they are
        all alike perverse;
    there is no one who does good,
    no, not one.

4 Have they no knowledge, those evildoers,

who eat up my people as they eat bread,
and do not call upon God?

⁵ There they shall be in great terror,
in terror such as has not been.
For God will scatter the bones of the ungodly;
they will be put to shame, for God
has rejected them.

⁶ O that deliverance for Israel would
come from Zion!
When God restores the fortunes
of his people,
Jacob will rejoice; Israel will be glad.

Psalm 54

To the leader: with stringed instruments.
A Maskil of David, when the Ziphites went and
told Saul, "David is hiding among us."

Save me, O God, by your name,
and vindicate me by your might.
² Hear my prayer, O God;
give ear to the words of my mouth.

³ For the insolent have risen against me,
the ruthless seek my life;
they do not set God before them.   Selah

⁴ But surely, God is my helper;
the Lord is the upholder of my life.
⁵ He will repay my enemies for their evil.
In your faithfulness, put an end to them.

⁶ With a freewill offering I will sacrifice to you;
I will give thanks to your name, O LORD,
for it is good.
⁷ For he has delivered me from every trouble,
and my eye has looked in triumph
on my enemies.

Psalm 55

To the leader: with stringed instruments.
A Maskil of David.

Give ear to my prayer, O God;
do not hide yourself from my supplication.
² Attend to me, and answer me;
I am troubled in my complaint.
I am distraught ³ by the noise of the enemy,
because of the clamor of the wicked.
For they bring trouble upon me,
and in anger they cherish enmity against me.

⁴ My heart is in anguish within me,
the terrors of death have fallen upon me.
⁵ Fear and trembling come upon me,
and horror overwhelms me.
⁶ And I say, "O that I had wings like a dove!
I would fly away and be at rest;
⁷ truly, I would flee far away;
I would lodge in the wilderness;   Selah
⁸ I would hurry to find a shelter for myself
from the raging wind and tempest."

⁹ Confuse, O Lord, confound their speech;
for I see violence and strife in the city.
¹⁰ Day and night they go around it
on its walls,
and iniquity and trouble are within it;
¹¹ ruin is in its midst;
oppression and fraud
do not depart from its marketplace.

¹² It is not enemies who taunt me —
I could bear that;
it is not adversaries who deal insolently
with me —
I could hide from them;
¹³ But it is you, my equal,
my companion, my familiar friend,
¹⁴ with whom I kept pleasant company;
we walked in the house of God
with the throng.
¹⁵ Let death come upon them;
let them go down alive to Sheol;
for evil is in their homes and in their hearts.

¹⁶ But I call upon God,
and the LORD will save me.
¹⁷ Evening and morning and at noon
I utter my complaint and moan,
and he will hear my voice.
¹⁸ He will redeem me unharmed
from the battle that I wage,
for many are arrayed against me.
¹⁹ God, who is enthroned from of old,   Selah
will hear, and will humble them —
because they do not change,
and do not fear God.

²⁰ My companion laid hands on a friend
and violated a covenant with me
²¹ with speech smoother than butter,
but with a heart set on war;
with words that were softer than oil,
but in fact were drawn swords.

f Cn Compare Gk Syr: Heb him
  who encamps against you
g Gk: Heb you have put [them]
  to shame
h Gk Syr Jerome: Heb
  is of those who uphold
  or is with those
  who uphold
i Cn Compare Gk: Heb
  they cause to totter
j Heb lacks with me

i Lament

22 Cast your burden on the LORD,
    and he will sustain you;
he will never permit
    the righteous to be moved.

23 But you, O God, will cast them down
    into the lowest pit;
the bloodthirsty and the treacherous
    shall not live out half their days.
But I will trust in you.

Psalm 56

*To the leader: according to The Dove on Far-off
Terebinths. Of David. A Miktam, when the
Philistines seized him in Gath.*

Be gracious to me, O God, for people
    trample on me;
    all day long foes oppress me;
2 my enemies trample on me all day long,
    for many fight against me.
O Most High, 3 when I am afraid,
    I put my trust in you.
4 In God, whose word I praise,
    in God I trust; I am not afraid;
    what can flesh do to me?

5 All day long they seek to injure my cause;
    all their thoughts are against me for evil.
6 They stir up strife, they lurk,
    they watch my steps.
As they hoped to have my life,
7   so repay them for their crime;
    in wrath cast down the peoples, O God!

8 You have kept count of my tossings;
    put my tears in your bottle.
    Are they not in your record?
9 Then my enemies will retreat
    in the day when I call.
    This I know, that God is for me.
10 In God, whose word I praise,
    in the LORD, whose word I praise,
11 in God I trust; I am not afraid.
    What can a mere mortal do to me?

12 My vows to you I must perform, O God;
    I will render thank offerings to you.
13 For you have delivered my soul from death,
    and my feet from falling,
    so that I may walk before God
    in the light of life.

*h Or Cast what he has
    given you
i Cn: Heb rescue
m Or because
n Cn: Heb are aflame for
o Or mighty lords*

1 Lament

Psalm 57

*To the leader: Do Not Destroy. Of David. A Miktam,
    when he fled from Saul, in the cave.*

Be merciful to me, O God, be merciful to me,
    for in you my soul takes refuge;
in the shadow of your wings I will take refuge,
    until the destroying storms pass by.
2 I cry to God Most High,
    to God who fulfills his purpose for me.
3 He will send from heaven and save me,
    he will put to shame those who
        trample on me.   Selah
God will send forth his steadfast love
    and his faithfulness.

4 I lie down among lions
    that greedily devour human prey;
their teeth are spears and arrows,
    their tongues sharp swords.

5 Be exalted, O God, above the heavens.
    Let your glory be over all the earth.

6 They set a net for my steps;
    my soul was bowed down.
They dug a pit in my path,
    but they have fallen into it themselves. Selah
7 My heart is steadfast, O God,
    my heart is steadfast.
I will sing and make melody.
8   Awake, my soul!
Awake, O harp and lyre!
    I will awake the dawn.
9 I will give thanks to you, O Lord,
    among the peoples;
    I will sing praises to you among the nations.
10 For your steadfast love is as high
        as the heavens;
    your faithfulness extends to the clouds.

11 Be exalted, O God, above the heavens.
    Let your glory be over all the earth.

Psalm 58

To the leader: Do Not Destroy. Of David. A Miktam.

Do you indeed decree what is right, you gods?
    Do you judge people fairly?
2 No, in your hearts you devise wrongs;
    your hands deal out violence on earth.

³ The wicked go astray from the womb;
  they err from their birth, speaking lies.
⁴ They have venom like the venom of a serpent,
  like the deaf adder that stops its ear,
⁵ so that it does not hear the voice of charmers
  or of the cunning enchanter.

⁶ O God, break the teeth in their mouths;
  tear out the fangs of the young lions, O LORD!
⁷ Let them vanish like water that runs away;
  like grass let them be trodden
    down and wither.
⁸ Let them be like the snail that
    dissolves into slime;
  like the untimely birth that never
    sees the sun.
⁹ Sooner than your pots can feel the
    heat of thorns,
  whether green or ablaze, may he
    sweep them away!

¹⁰ The righteous will rejoice when they see
    vengeance done;
  they will bathe their feet in the blood
    of the wicked.
¹¹ People will say, "Surely there is a reward
    for the righteous;
  surely there is a God who judges on earth."

Psalm 59

To the leader: Do Not Destroy. Of David.
A Miktam, when Saul ordered his house to be
watched in order to kill him.

Deliver me from my enemies, O my God;
  protect me from those who rise
    up against me.
² Deliver me from those who work evil;
  from the bloodthirsty save me.

³ Even now they lie in wait for my life;
  the mighty stir up strife against me.
⁴ For no transgression or sin of mine, O LORD,
  for no fault of mine, they run
    and make ready.

Rouse yourself, come to my help and see!
⁵   You, LORD God of hosts, are God of Israel.
  Awake to punish all the nations;
    spare none of those who treacherously
      plot evil.   Selah

⁶ Each evening they come back,
  howling like dogs

and prowling about the city.
⁷ There they are, bellowing with their mouths,
  with sharp words on their lips —
    for "Who," they think, "will hear us?"

⁸ But you laugh at them, O LORD;
  you hold all the nations in derision.
⁹ O my strength, I will watch for you;
  for you, O God, are my fortress.
¹⁰ My God in his steadfast love will meet me;
  my God will let me look in triumph
    on my enemies.

¹¹ Do not kill them, or my people may forget;
  make them totter by your power,
    and bring them down,
    O Lord, our shield.
¹² For the sin of their mouths, the
    words of their lips,
  let them be trapped in their pride.
  For the cursing and lies that they utter,
¹³   consume them in wrath;
  consume them until they are no more.
  Then it will be known to the ends of the earth
    that God rules over Jacob.   Selah

¹⁴ Each evening they come back,
    howling like dogs
  and prowling about the city.
¹⁵ They roam about for food,
  and growl if they do not get their fill.

¹⁶ But I will sing of your might;
  I will sing aloud of your steadfast
    love in the morning.
  For you have been a fortress for me
    and a refuge in the day of my distress.
¹⁷ O my strength, I will sing praises to you,
  for you, O God, are my fortress,
    the God who shows me steadfast love.

Psalm 60

To the leader: according to the Lily of the
Covenant. A Miktam of David; for instruction;
when he struggled with Aram-naharaim
and with Aram-zobah, and when Joab on his
return killed twelve thousand Edomites in the
Valley of Salt.

O God, you have rejected us,
    broken our defenses;
  you have been angry; now restore us!
² You have caused the land to quake; you
    have torn it open;
  repair the cracks in it, for it is tottering.

ᵖ Cn: Meaning of Heb
  uncertain
ᵠ Heb with swords
ʳ Heb lacks they think

t Lament

3 You have made your people suffer hard things;
   you have given us wine to drink
      that made us reel.

4 You have set up a banner for those
      who fear you,
   to rally to it out of bowshot.   Selah
5 Give victory with your right hand,
      and answer us,
   so that those whom you love may be rescued.

6 God has promised in his sanctuary:
   "With exultation I will divide up Shechem,
      and portion out the Vale of Succoth.
7 Gilead is mine, and Manasseh is mine;
   Ephraim is my helmet;
   Judah is my scepter.
8 Moab is my washbasin;
   on Edom I hurl my shoe;
   over Philistia I shout in triumph."

9 Who will bring me to the fortified city?
   Who will lead me to Edom?
10 Have you not rejected us, O God?
   You do not go out, O God, with our armies.
11 O grant us help against the foe,
   for human help is worthless.
12 With God we shall do valiantly;
   it is he who will tread down our foes.

Psalm 61

To the leader:
with stringed instruments. Of David.

Hear my cry, O God;
   listen to my prayer.
2 From the end of the earth I call to you,
   when my heart is faint.

   Lead me to the rock
      that is higher than I;
3 for you are my refuge,
   a strong tower against the enemy.

4 Let me abide in your tent forever,
   find refuge under the shelter
      of your wings.   Selah
5 For you, O God, have heard my vows;
   you have given me the heritage of those
      who fear your name.

6 Prolong the life of the king;
   may his years endure to all generations!

s Gk Syr Jerome: Heb
   because of the truth
t Another reading is me
u Or by his holiness

I Lament
IV Confidence

7 May he be enthroned forever before God;
   appoint steadfast love and faithfulness to
      watch over him!

8 So I will always sing praises to your name,
   as I pay my vows day after day.

IV Psalm 62

To the leader: according to Jeduthun.
A Psalm of David.

For God alone my soul waits in silence;
   from him comes my salvation.
2 He alone is my rock and my salvation,
   my fortress; I shall never be shaken.

3 How long will you assail a person,
   will you batter your victim, all of you,
      as would a leaning wall,
         a tottering fence?
4 Their only plan is to bring down a
      person of prominence.
   They take pleasure in falsehood;
   they bless with their mouths,
      but inwardly they curse.   Selah

5 For God alone my soul waits in silence,
   for my hope is from him.
6 He alone is my rock and my salvation,
   my fortress; I shall not be shaken.
7 On God rests my deliverance and my honor;
   my mighty rock, my refuge is in God.

8 Trust in him at all times, O people;
   pour out your heart before him;
   God is a refuge for us.   Selah

9 Those of low estate are but a breath,
   those of high estate are a delusion;
   in the balances they go up;
   they are together lighter than a breath.
10 Put no confidence in extortion,
   and set no vain hopes on robbery;
   if riches increase, do not set your
      heart on them.

11 Once God has spoken;
   twice have I heard this:
   that power belongs to God,
12   and steadfast love belongs to you, O Lord.
   For you repay to all
      according to their work.

Psalm 63

A Psalm of David, when he was in the Wilderness of Judah.

O God, you are my God, I seek you,
    my soul thirsts for you;
my flesh faints for you,
    as in a dry and weary land
        where there is no water.
2 So I have looked upon you in the sanctuary,
    beholding your power and glory.
3 Because your steadfast love is better than life,
    my lips will praise you.
4 So I will bless you as long as I live;
    I will lift up my hands and call on your name.

5 My soul is satisfied as with a rich feast,
    and my mouth praises you with joyful lips
6 when I think of you on my bed,
    and meditate on you in the watches
        of the night;
7 for you have been my help,
    and in the shadow of your wings
        I sing for joy.
8 My soul clings to you;
    your right hand upholds me.

9 But those who seek to destroy my life
    shall go down into the depths of the earth;
10 they shall be given over to the power
        of the sword,
    they shall be prey for jackals.
11 But the king shall rejoice in God;
    all who swear by him shall exult,
    for the mouths of liars will be stopped.

Psalm 64

To the leader. A Psalm of David.

Hear my voice, O God, in my complaint;
    preserve my life from the dread enemy.
2 Hide me from the secret plots of the wicked,
    from the scheming of evildoers,
3 who whet their tongues like swords,
    who aim bitter words like arrows,
4 shooting from ambush at the blameless;
    they shoot suddenly and without fear.
5 They hold fast to their evil purpose;
    they talk of laying snares secretly,
    thinking, "Who can see us?
6   Who can search out our crimes?
We have thought out a cunningly
        conceived plot."

For the human heart and mind are deep.

7 But God will shoot his arrow at them;
    they will be wounded suddenly.
8 Because of their tongue he will bring
        them to ruin;
    all who see them will shake with horror.
9 Then everyone will fear;
    they will tell what God has brought about,
    and ponder what he has done.

10 Let the righteous rejoice in the LORD
    and take refuge in him.
Let all the upright in heart glory.

Psalm 65

To the leader. A Psalm of David. A Song.

Praise is due to you,
    O God, in Zion;
and to you shall vows be performed,
2   O you who answer prayer!
To you all flesh shall come.
3 When deeds of iniquity overwhelm us,
    you forgive our transgressions.
4 Happy are those whom you choose
        and bring near
    to live in your courts.
We shall be satisfied with the goodness
        of your house,
    your holy temple.

5 By awesome deeds you answer us
        with deliverance,
    O God of our salvation;
you are the hope of all the ends of the earth
    and of the farthest seas.
6 By your strength you established
        the mountains;
    you are girded with might.
7 You silence the roaring of the seas,
    the roaring of their waves,
    the tumult of the peoples.
8 Those who live at earth's farthest bounds
    are awed by your signs;
you make the gateways of the morning
    and the evening shout for joy.

9 You visit the earth and water it,
    you greatly enrich it;
the river of God is full of water;
    you provide the people with grain,
    for so you have prepared it.

* Heb *with fat and fatness*
" Syr: Heb *them*
× Cn: Heb *They search out crimes*
γ Cn: Heb *They will bring him to ruin, their tongue bring against them*
ƶ Gk Jerome: Heb *his*

IV Confidence
I Lament
III Thanksgiving

¹⁰ You water its furrows abundantly,
      settling its ridges,
   softening it with showers,
      and blessing its growth.
¹¹ You crown the year with your bounty;
      your wagon tracks overflow with richness.
¹² The pastures of the wilderness overflow,
      the hills gird themselves with joy,
¹³ the meadows clothe themselves with flocks,
      the valleys deck themselves with grain,
      they shout and sing together for joy.

II·III Psalm 66

To the leader. A Song. A Psalm.

Make a joyful noise to God, all the earth;
²   sing the glory of his name;
      give to him glorious praise.
³ Say to God, "How awesome are your deeds!
      Because of your great power, your enemies
         cringe before you.
⁴ All the earth worships you;
      they sing praises to you,
      sing praises to your name."   Selah

⁵ Come and see what God has done:
      he is awesome in his deeds among mortals.
⁶ He turned the sea into dry land;
      they passed through the river on foot.
   There we rejoiced in him,
⁷   who rules by his might forever,
   whose eyes keep watch on the nations —
      let the rebellious not exalt themselves.   Selah

⁸ Bless our God, O peoples,
      let the sound of his praise be heard,
⁹ who has kept us among the living,
      and has not let our feet slip.
¹⁰ For you, O God, have tested us;
      you have tried us as silver is tried.
¹¹ You brought us into the net;
      you laid burdens on our backs;
¹² you let people ride over our heads;
      we went through fire and through water;
   yet you have brought us out to
         a spacious place.ᵃ

¹³ I will come into your house with
         burnt offerings;
   I will pay you my vows,
¹⁴ those that my lips uttered
      and my mouth promised when
         I was in trouble.

ᵃ Cn Compare Gk Syr
   Jerome Tg: Heb *to a*
      saturation

II Hymn [Psalm 66 v.1-12]
III Thanksgiving [Psalm 66 v.13-20]
VI Liturgy

¹⁵ I will offer to you burnt offerings of fatlings,
      with the smoke of the sacrifice of rams;
   I will make an offering of bulls and goats.
                                             Selah

¹⁶ Come and hear, all you who fear God,
      and I will tell what he has done for me.
¹⁷ I cried aloud to him,
      and he was extolled with my tongue.
¹⁸ If I had cherished iniquity in my heart,
      the Lord would not have listened.
¹⁹ But truly God has listened;
      he has given heed to the words of my prayer.

²⁰ Blessed be God,
      because he has not rejected my prayer
      or removed his steadfast love from me.

VI Psalm 67

To the leader: with stringed instruments.
A Psalm. A Song.

May God be gracious to us and bless us
      and make his face to shine upon us,   Selah
²   that your way may be known upon earth,
      your saving power among all nations.
³ Let the peoples praise you, O God;
      let all the peoples praise you.

⁴ Let the nations be glad and sing for joy,
      for you judge the peoples with equity
      and guide the nations upon earth.   Selah
⁵ Let the peoples praise you, O God;
      let all the peoples praise you.

⁶ The earth has yielded its increase;
      God, our God, has blessed us.
⁷ May God continue to bless us;
      let all the ends of the earth revere him.

VI Psalm 68

To the leader. Of David. A Psalm. A Song.

Let God rise up, let his enemies be scattered;
      let those who hate him flee before him.
² As smoke is driven away, so drive them away;
      as wax melts before the fire,
      let the wicked perish before God.
³ But let the righteous be joyful;
      let them exult before God;
      let them be jubilant with joy.

4 Sing to God, sing praises to his name;
   lift up a song to him who rides
      upon the clouds —
   his name is the LORD —
   be exultant before him.

5 Father of orphans and protector of widows
   is God in his holy habitation.
6 God gives the desolate a home to live in;
   he leads out the prisoners to prosperity,
   but the rebellious live in a parched land.

7 O God, when you went out before your people,
   when you marched through
      the wilderness,   Selah
8 the earth quaked, the heavens
      poured down rain
   at the presence of God, the God of Sinai,
   at the presence of God, the God of Israel.
9 Rain in abundance, O God, you
      showered abroad;
   you restored your heritage when
      it languished;
10 your flock found a dwelling in it;
   in your goodness, O God, you
      provided for the needy.

11 The Lord gives the command;
   great is the company of those who
      bore the tidings;
12 "The kings of the armies, they flee,
      they flee!"
   The women at home divide the spoil,
13 though they stay among the sheepfolds —
   the wings of a dove covered with silver,
   its pinions with green gold.
14 When the Almighty scattered kings there,
   snow fell on Zalmon.

15 O mighty mountain, mountain of Bashan;
   O many-peaked mountain,
      mountain of Bashan!
16 Why do you look with envy,
      O many-peaked mountain,
   at the mount that God desired for his abode,
   where the LORD will reside forever?

17 With mighty chariotry, twice ten thousand,
   thousands upon thousands,
   the Lord came from Sinai into
      the holy place.
18 You ascended the high mount,
   leading captives in your train
   and receiving gifts from people,

even from those who rebel against the LORD
      God's abiding there.
19 Blessed be the Lord,
   who daily bears us up;
   God is our salvation.   Selah
20 Our God is a God of salvation,
   and to God, the Lord, belongs
      escape from death.

21 But God will shatter the heads of his enemies,
   the hairy crown of those who walk
      in their guilty ways.
22 The Lord said,
   "I will bring them back from Bashan,
   I will bring them back from the
      depths of the sea,
23 so that you may bathe your feet in blood,
   so that the tongues of your dogs may have
      their share from the foe."

24 Your solemn processions are seen, O God,
   the processions of my God, my King,
      into the sanctuary —
25 the singers in front, the musicians last,
   between them girls playing tambourines:
26 "Bless God in the great congregation,
   the LORD, O you who are of Israel's fountain!"
27 There is Benjamin, the least of them,
      in the lead,
   the princes of Judah in a body,
   the princes of Zebulun, the
      princes of Naphtali,

28 Summon your might, O God;
   show your strength, O God, as you have
      done for us before.
29 Because of your temple at Jerusalem
   kings bear gifts to you.
30 Rebuke the wild animals that live
      among the reeds,
   the herd of bulls with the calves
      of the peoples.
   Trample under foot those who
      lust after tribute;
   scatter the peoples who delight in war.
31 Let bronze be brought from Egypt;
   let Ethiopia hasten to stretch out its
      hands to God.

32 Sing to God, O kingdoms of the earth;
   sing praises to the Lord,   Selah
33 O rider in the heavens, the ancient heavens;
   listen, he sends out his voice,
      his mighty voice.

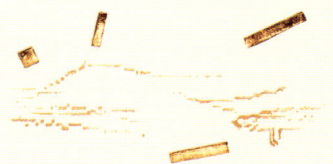

b Or cast up a highway for
  him who rides through the
  deserts
c Or company of the
  women
d Traditional rendering of
  Heb Shaddai
e Cn: Heb The Lord among
  them Sinai in the holy
  [place]
f Gk Syr Tg: Heb shatter
g Or have been seen
h Cn: Heb Trampling
i Meaning of Heb of
  verse 30 is uncertain
j Or Nubia: Heb Cush

34 Ascribe power to God,
  whose majesty is over Israel;
  and whose power is in the skies.
35 Awesome is God in his sanctuary,
  the God of Israel;
  he gives power and strength to his people.

Blessed be God!

Psalm 69

(To the leader: according to Lilies. Of David.

Save me, O God,
  for the waters have come up to my neck.
2 I sink in deep mire,
  where there is no foothold;
I have come into deep waters,
  and the flood sweeps over me.
3 I am weary with my crying;
  my throat is parched.
My eyes grow dim
  with waiting for my God.

4 More in number than the hairs of my head
  are those who hate me without cause;
many are those who would destroy me,
  my enemies who accuse me falsely.
What I did not steal
  must I now restore?
5 O God, you know my folly;
  the wrongs I have done are not
    hidden from you.

6 Do not let those who hope in you be put to
    shame because of me,
  O Lord GOD of hosts;
do not let those who seek you be
    dishonored because of me,
  O God of Israel.
7 It is for your sake that I have borne reproach,
  that shame has covered my face.
8 I have become a stranger to my kindred,
  an alien to my mother's children.

9 It is zeal for your house that has consumed me;
  the insults of those who insult you
    have fallen on me.
10 When I humbled my soul with fasting,
  they insulted me for doing so.
11 When I made sackcloth my clothing,
  I became a byword to them.
12 I am the subject of gossip for those
    who sit in the gate,

and the drunkards make songs about me.

13 But as for me, my prayer is to you, O LORD.
  At an acceptable time, O God,
  in the abundance of your steadfast love,
    answer me.
With your faithful help 14 rescue me
  from sinking in the mire;
let me be delivered from my enemies
  and from the deep waters.
15 Do not let the flood sweep over me,
  or the deep swallow me up,
  or the Pit close its mouth over me.

16 Answer me, O LORD, for your
    steadfast love is good;
  according to your abundant mercy,
    turn to me.
17 Do not hide your face from your servant,
  for I am in distress — make haste
    to answer me.
18 Draw near to me, redeem me,
  set me free because of my enemies.

19 You know the insults I receive,
  and my shame and dishonor;
  my foes are all known to you.
20 Insults have broken my heart,
  so that I am in despair.
I looked for pity, but there was none;
  and for comforters, but I found none.
21 They gave me poison for food,
  and for my thirst they gave me
    vinegar to drink.

22 Let their table be a trap for them,
  a snare for their allies.
23 Let their eyes be darkened so that
    they cannot see,
  and make their loins tremble continually.
24 Pour out your indignation upon them,
  and let your burning anger overtake them.
25 May their camp be a desolation;
  let no one live in their tents.
26 For they persecute those whom you
    have struck down,
  and those whom you have wounded,
    they attack still more.
27 Add guilt to their guilt;
  may they have no acquittal from you.
28 Let them be blotted out of the
    book of the living;
  let them not be enrolled among
    the righteous.

²⁹ But I am lowly and in pain;
   let your salvation, O God, protect me.

³⁰ I will praise the name of God with a song;
   I will magnify him with thanksgiving.
³¹ This will please the LORD more than an ox
   or a bull with horns and hoofs.
³² Let the oppressed see it and be glad:
   you who seek God, let your hearts revive.
³³ For the LORD hears the needy,
   and does not despise his own
      that are in bonds.

³⁴ Let heaven and earth praise him,
   the seas and everything that moves in them.
³⁵ For God will save Zion
   and rebuild the cities of Judah;
   and his servants shall live there and possess it;
³⁶ the children of his servants shall inherit it,
   and those who love his name shall live in it.

Psalm 70

To the leader. Of David, for the memorial offering.

Be pleased, O God, to deliver me.
   O LORD, make haste to help me!
² Let those be put to shame and confusion
   who seek my life.
Let those be turned back and brought
      to dishonor
   who desire to hurt me.
³ Let those who say, "Aha, Aha!"
   turn back because of their shame.

⁴ Let all who seek you
   rejoice and be glad in you.
Let those who love your salvation
   say evermore, "God is great!"
⁵ But I am poor and needy;
   hasten to me, O God!
You are my help and my deliverer;
   O LORD, do not delay!

Psalm 71

In you, O LORD, I take refuge;
   let me never be put to shame.
² In your righteousness deliver me
      and rescue me;
   incline your ear to me and save me.
³ Be to me a rock of refuge,
   a strong fortress, to save me,

for you are my rock and my fortress.

⁴ Rescue me, O my God, from the hand
      of the wicked,
   from the grasp of the unjust and cruel.
⁵ For you, O Lord, are my hope,
   my trust, O LORD, from my youth.
⁶ Upon you I have leaned from my birth;
   it was you who took me from
      my mother's womb.
My praise is continually of you.

⁷ I have been like a portent to many,
   but you are my strong refuge.
⁸ My mouth is filled with your praise,
   and with your glory all day long.
⁹ Do not cast me off in the time of old age;
   do not forsake me when my strength is spent.
¹⁰ For my enemies speak concerning me,
   and those who watch for my
      life consult together.
¹¹ They say, "Pursue and seize that person
   whom God has forsaken,
   for there is no one to deliver."

¹² O God, do not be far from me;
   O my God, make haste to help me!
¹³ Let my accusers be put to shame
      and consumed;
   let those who seek to hurt me
   be covered with scorn and disgrace.
¹⁴ But I will hope continually,
   and will praise you yet more and more.
¹⁵ My mouth will tell of your righteous acts,
   of your deeds of salvation all day long,
      though their number is past my knowledge.
¹⁶ I will come praising the mighty deeds
      of the Lord GOD,
   I will praise your righteousness, yours alone.

¹⁷ O God, from my youth you have taught me,
   and I still proclaim your wondrous deeds.
¹⁸ So even to old age and gray hairs,
   O God, do not forsake me,
until I proclaim your might
   to all the generations to come.
Your power ¹⁹ and your righteousness, O God,
   reach the high heavens.

You who have done great things,
   O God, who is like you?
²⁰ You who have made me see many
      troubles and calamities
   will revive me again;

RSB
Psalm 70:1

ⁿ Syr: Heb *and they shall live*
ᵒ Gk Compare 31.3 Heb *to come*
   continually you have
   commanded
ᵖ Gk Compare Syr: Heb *to a*
   generation, to all that come

1 Lament

from the depths of the earth
    you will bring me up again.
²¹ You will increase my honor,
    and comfort me once again.

²² I will also praise you with the harp
    for your faithfulness, O my God;
I will sing praises to you with the lyre,
    O Holy One of Israel.
²³ My lips will shout for joy
    when I sing praises to you;
    my soul also, which you have rescued.
²⁴ All day long my tongue will talk of
    your righteous help,
for those who tried to do me harm
    have been put to shame, and disgraced.

ᵛᴵᴵ Psalm 72

Of Solomon.

Give the king your justice, O God,
    and your righteousness to a king's son.
² May he judge your people with righteousness,
    and your poor with justice.
³ May the mountains yield prosperity
    for the people,
    and the hills, in righteousness.
⁴ May he defend the cause of the
    poor of the people,
    give deliverance to the needy,
    and crush the oppressor.

⁵ May he live while the sun endures,
    and as long as the moon, throughout
      all generations.
⁶ May he be like rain that falls on
    the mown grass,
    like showers that water the earth.
⁷ In his days may righteousness flourish
    and peace abound, until the
      moon is no more.

⁸ May he have dominion from sea to sea,
    and from the River to the ends of the earth.
⁹ May his foes bow down before him,
    and his enemies lick the dust.
¹⁰ May the kings of Tarshish and of the isles
    render him tribute,
may the kings of Sheba and Seba
    bring gifts.
¹¹ May all kings fall down before him,
    all nations give him service.

¹² For he delivers the needy when they call,
    the poor and those who have no helper.
¹³ He has pity on the weak and the needy,
    and saves the lives of the needy.
¹⁴ From oppression and violence he
     redeems their life;
    and precious is their blood in his sight.

¹⁵ Long may he live!
    May gold of Sheba be given to him.
May prayer be made for him continually,
    and blessings invoked for him all day long.
¹⁶ May there be abundance of grain in the land;
    may it wave on the tops of the mountains;
    may its fruit be like Lebanon;
and may people blossom in the cities
    like the grass of the field.
¹⁷ May his name endure forever,
    his fame continue as long as the sun.
May all nations be blessed in him;
    may they pronounce him happy.

¹⁸ Blessed be the LORD, the God of Israel,
    who alone does wondrous things.
¹⁹ Blessed be his glorious name forever;
    may his glory fill the whole earth.

Amen & Amen

²⁰ The prayers of David son of Jesse are ended.

Psalm 73

A Psalm of Asaph.

Truly God is good to the upright;
  to those who are pure in heart.
2 But as for me, my feet had almost stumbled;
  my steps had nearly slipped.
3 For I was envious of the arrogant;
  I saw the prosperity of the wicked.

4 For they have no pain;
  their bodies are sound and sleek.
5 They are not in trouble as others are;
  they are not plagued like other people.
6 Therefore pride is their necklace;
  violence covers them like a garment.
7 Their eyes swell out with fatness;
  their hearts overflow with follies.
8 They scoff and speak with malice;
  loftily they threaten oppression.
9 They set their mouths against heaven,
  and their tongues range over the earth.

10 Therefore the people turn and praise them,
  and find no fault in them.
11 And they say, "How can God know?
  Is there knowledge in the Most High?"
12 Such are the wicked;
  always at ease, they increase in riches.
13 All in vain I have kept my heart clean
  and washed my hands in innocence.
14 For all day long I have been plagued,
  and am punished every morning.

15 If I had said, "I will talk on in this way,"
  I would have been untrue to the circle
    of your children.
16 But when I thought how to understand this,
  it seemed to me a wearisome task,
17 until I went into the sanctuary of God;
  then I perceived their end.
18 Truly you set them in slippery places;
  you make them fall to ruin.
19 How they are destroyed in a moment,
  swept away utterly by terrors!
20 They are like a dream when one awakes;
  on awaking you despise their phantoms.

21 When my soul was embittered,
  when I was pricked in heart,
22 I was stupid and ignorant;
  I was like a brute beast toward you.
23 Nevertheless I am continually with you;
  you hold my right hand.

BOOK III

t Or good to Israel
u Cn: Heb his people return here
v Cn: Heb abundant waters are drained by them
w Cn: Heb Lord

v Wisdom

²⁴ You guide me with your counsel,
    and afterward you will receive me
      with honor.
²⁵ Whom have I in heaven but you?
    And there is nothing on earth that I
      desire other than you.
²⁶ My flesh and my heart may fail,
    but God is the strength of my heart
      and my portion forever.

²⁷ Indeed, those who are far from you will perish;
    you put an end to those who are false to you.
²⁸ But for me it is good to be near God;
    I have made the Lord GOD my refuge,
    to tell of all your works.

Psalm 74

A Maskil of Asaph.

O God, why do you cast us off forever?
    Why does your anger smoke against the
      sheep of your pasture?
² Remember your congregation, which
      you acquired long ago,
    which you redeemed to be the tribe
      of your heritage.
    Remember Mount Zion, where you
      came to dwell.
³ Direct your steps to the perpetual ruins;
    the enemy has destroyed everything
      in the sanctuary.

⁴ Your foes have roared within your holy place;
    they set up their emblems there.
⁵ At the upper entrance they hacked
    the wooden trellis with axes.
⁶ And then, with hatchets and hammers,
    they smashed all its carved work.
⁷ They set your sanctuary on fire;
    they desecrated the dwelling place
      of your name,
    bringing it to the ground.
⁸ They said to themselves, "We will utterly
      subdue them";
    they burned all the meeting places
      of God in the land.

⁹ We do not see our emblems;
    there is no longer any prophet,
    and there is no one among us who
      knows how long.
¹⁰ How long, O God, is the foe to scoff?
    Is the enemy to revile your name forever?

^a Or *in glory*
^b Heb *neck*
^c Cn Compare Gk Syr:
  Meaning of Heb uncertain
^d Cn: Heb *do you consume
  your right hand from*
^e Heb *food for the people*
^f Or *moon*: Heb *halts*
^g Gk Syr: Heb *the*

^I Lament
^{III} Thanksgiving

¹¹ Why do you hold back your hand;
    why do you keep your hand in your bosom?

¹² Yet God my King is from of old,
    working salvation in the earth.
¹³ You divided the sea by your might;
    you broke the heads of the
      dragons in the waters.
¹⁴ You crushed the heads of Leviathan;
    you gave him as food for the creatures
      of the wilderness.
¹⁵ You cut openings for springs and torrents;
    you dried up ever-flowing streams.
¹⁶ Yours is the day, yours also the night;
    you established the luminaries and the sun.
¹⁷ You have fixed all the bounds of the earth;
    you made summer and winter.

¹⁸ Remember this, O LORD, how the enemy scoffs,
    and an impious people reviles your name.
¹⁹ Do not deliver the soul of your dove
      to the wild animals;
    do not forget the life of your poor forever.

²⁰ Have regard for your covenant,
    for the dark places of the land are full of
      the haunts of violence.
²¹ Do not let the downtrodden be put to shame;
    let the poor and needy praise your name.
²² Rise up, O God, plead your cause;
    remember how the impious scoff at
      you all day long.
²³ Do not forget the clamor of your foes,
    the uproar of your adversaries that
      goes up continually.

^{III} Psalm 75

To the leader: Do Not Destroy. A Psalm of Asaph. A Song.

We give thanks to you, O God;
    we give thanks; your name is near.
    People tell of your wondrous deeds.

² At the set time that I appoint
    I will judge with equity.
³ When the earth totters, with all its inhabitants,
    it is I who keep its pillars steady.   *Selah*
⁴ I say to the boastful, "Do not boast,"
    and to the wicked, "Do not lift up your horn;
⁵ do not lift up your horn on high,
    or speak with insolent neck."

6 For not from the east or from the west
   and not from the wilderness
      comes lifting up;
7 but it is God who executes judgment,
   putting down one and lifting up another.
 For in the hand of the LORD there is a cup
   with foaming wine, well mixed;
8 he will pour a draught from it,
   and all the wicked of the earth
      shall drain it down to the dregs.
9 But I will rejoice forever;
   I will sing praises to the God of Jacob.

10 All the horns of the wicked I will cut off,
   but the horns of the righteous
      shall be exalted.

Psalm 76

To the leader: with stringed instruments.
A Psalm of Asaph. A Song.

 In Judah God is known,
   his name is great in Israel.
2 His abode has been established in Salem,
   his dwelling place in Zion.
3 There he broke the flashing arrows,
   the shield, the sword, and the
      weapons of war.   *Selah*

4 Glorious are you, more majestic
   than the everlasting mountains.
5 The stouthearted were stripped of their spoil;
   they sank into sleep;
 none of the troops
   was able to lift a hand.
6 At your rebuke, O God of Jacob,
   both rider and horse lay stunned.

7 But you indeed are awesome!
   Who can stand before you
      when once your anger is roused?
8 From the heavens you uttered judgment;
   the earth feared and was still
9 when God rose up to establish judgment,
   to save all the oppressed of the earth.   *Selah*

10 Human wrath serves only to praise you,
   when you bind the last bit of your
      wrath around you.
11 Make vows to the LORD your God,
   and perform them;
 let all who are around him bring gifts
   to the one who is awesome,

12 who cuts off the spirit of princes,
   who inspires fear in the kings of the earth.

Psalm 77

To the leader: According to Jeduthun. Of Asaph.
A Psalm.

 I cry aloud to God,
   aloud to God, that he may hear me.
2 In the day of trouble I seek the Lord;
   in the night my hand is stretched out
      without wearying;
 my soul refuses to be comforted.
3 I think of God, and moan;
   I meditate, and my spirit faints.   *Selah*

4 You keep my eyelids from closing;
   I am so troubled that I cannot speak.
5 I consider the days of old,
   and remember the years of long ago.
6 I commune with my heart in the night;
   I meditate and search my spirit:
7 "Will the Lord spurn forever,
   and never again be favorable?
8 Has his steadfast love ceased forever?
   Are his promises at an end for all time?
9 Has God forgotten to be gracious?
   Has he in anger shut up
      his compassion?"   *Selah*

10 And I say, "It is my grief
   that the right hand of the Most High
      has changed."

11 I will call to mind the deeds of the LORD;
   I will remember your wonders of old.
12 I will meditate on all your work,
   and muse on your mighty deeds.
13 Your way, O God, is holy.
   What god is so great as our God?
14 You are the God who works wonders;
   you have displayed your might
      among the peoples.
15 With your strong arm you redeemed
   your people,
      the descendants of Jacob and Joseph.   *Selah*

16 When the waters saw you, O God,
   when the waters saw you, they were afraid;
      the very deep trembled.
17 The clouds poured out water;
   the skies thundered;
 your arrows flashed on every side.
18 The crash of your thunder was

RSB
Psalm 76:10

e Gk: Heb *declare*
f Gk: Heb *the mountains of prey*
g Heb lacks *your*
h Gk Syr: Heb *My music*
i Syr Jerome: Heb *my spirit searches*

VIII Zion Songs
I Lament

in the whirlwind;
yourlightnings lit up the world;
the earth trembled and shook.
19 Vour way was through the sea,
your path, through the mighty waters;
yet your footprints were unseen.
20 You led your people like a flock
by the hand of Moses and Aaron.

Psalm 78

A Maskil of Asaph.

Give ear, O my people, to my teaching;
incline your ears to the words of my mouth.
2 I will open my mouth in a parable;
I will utter dark sayings from of old,
3 things that we have heard and known,
that our ancestors have told us.
4 We will not hide them from their children;
we will tell the coming generation
the glorious deeds of the LORD, and his might,
and the wonders that he has done.

5 He established a decree in Jacob,
and appointed a law in Israel,
which he commanded our ancestors
to teach to their children;
6 that the next generation might know them,
the children yet unborn,
and rise up and tell them to their children,
7 so that they should set their hope in God,
and not forget the works of God,
but keep his commandments;
8 and that they should not be
like their ancestors,
a stubborn and rebellious generation,
a generation whose heart was not steadfast,
whose spirit was not faithful to God.

9 The Ephraimites, armed with the bow,
turned back on the day of battle.
10 They did not keep God's covenant,
but refused to walk according to his law.
11 They forgot what he had done,
and the miracles that he had shown them.
12 In the sight of their ancestors
he worked marvels
in the land of Egypt, in the fields of Zoan.
13 He divided the sea and let them
pass through it,
and made the waters stand like a heap.
14 In the daytime he led them with a cloud,
and all night long with a fiery light.

15 He split rocks open in the wilderness,
and gave them drink abundantly
as from the deep.
16 He made streams come out of the rock,
and caused waters to flow down like rivers.

17 Yet they sinned still more against him,
rebelling against the Most High in the desert.
18 They tested God in their heart
by demanding the food they craved.
19 They spoke against God saying,
"Can God spread a table in the wilderness?
20 Even though he struck the rock so that
water rushed out
and torrents overflowed,
can he also give bread,
or provide meat for his people?"

21 Therefore, when the LORD heard,
he was full of rage;
a fire was kindled against Jacob,
his anger mounted against Israel,
22 because they had no faith in God,
and did not trust his saving power.
23 Yet he commanded the skies above,
and opened the doors of heaven;
24 he rained down on them manna to eat,
and gave them the grain of heaven.
25 Mortals ate of the bread of angels;
he sent them food in abundance.
26 He caused the east wind to blow
in the heavens,
and by his power he led out the south wind;
27 he rained flesh upon them like dust,
winged birds fell like the sand of the seas;
28 he let them fall within their camp,
all around their dwellings.
29 And they ate and were well filled,
for he gave them what they craved.
30 But before they had satisfied their craving,
while the food was still in their mouths,
31 the anger of God rose against them
and killed the strongest of them,
and laid low the flower of Israel.

32 In spite of all this they still sinned;
they did not believe in his wonders.
33 So he made their days vanish like a breath,
and their years in terror.
34 When he killed them, they sought for him;
they repented and sought God earnestly.
35 They remembered that God was their rock,
the Most High God their redeemer.
36 But they flattered him with their mouths;

Heb armed with shooting

IX Historical

they lied to him with their tongues.
37 Their heart was not steadfast toward him;
they were not true to his covenant.
38 Yet he, being compassionate,
forgave their iniquity,
and did not destroy them:
often he restrained his anger,
and did not stir up all his wrath.
39 He remembered that they were but flesh,
a wind that passes and does not come again.
40 How often they rebelled against
him in the wilderness
and grieved him in the desert!
41 They tested God again and again,
and provoked the Holy One of Israel.
42 They did not keep in mind his power,
or the day when he redeemed
them from the foe;
43 when he displayed his signs in Egypt,
and his miracles in the fields of Zoan.
44 He turned their rivers to blood,
so that they could not drink of their streams.
45 He sent among them swarms of flies,
which devoured them,
and frogs, which destroyed them.
46 He gave their crops to the caterpillar,
and the fruit of their labor to the locust.
47 He destroyed their vines with hail,
and their sycamores with frost.
48 He gave over their cattle to the hail,
and their flocks to thunderbolts.
49 He let loose on them his fierce anger,
wrath, indignation, and distress,
a company of destroying angels.
50 He made a path for his anger;
he did not spare them from death,
but gave their lives over to the plague.
51 He struck all the firstborn in Egypt,
the first issue of their strength
in the tents of Ham.
52 Then he led out his people like sheep,
and guided them in the wilderness
like a flock.
53 He led them in safety so that they
were not afraid;
but the sea overwhelmed their enemies.
54 And he brought them to his holy hill,
to the mountain that his right hand had won.
55 He drove out nations before them;
he apportioned them for a possession
and settled the tribes of Israel in their tents.

56 Yet they tested the Most High God,
and rebelled against him.

They did not observe his decrees,
57 but turned away and were faithless
like their ancestors;
they twisted like a treacherous bow.
58 For they provoked him to anger
with their high places;
59 they moved him to jealousy with their idols.
When God heard, he was full of wrath,
and he utterly rejected Israel.
60 He abandoned his dwelling at Shiloh,
the tent where he dwelt among mortals,
61 and delivered his power to captivity,
his glory to the hand of the foe.
62 He gave his people to the sword,
and vented his wrath on his heritage.
63 Fire devoured their young men,
and their girls had no marriage song.
64 Their priests fell by the sword,
and their widows made no lamentation.
65 Then the Lord awoke as from sleep,
like a warrior shouting because of wine.
66 He put his adversaries to rout;
he put them to everlasting disgrace.

67 He rejected the tent of Joseph,
he did not choose the tribe of Ephraim;
68 but he chose the tribe of Judah,
Mount Zion, which he loves.
69 He built his sanctuary like the high heavens,
like the earth, which he has founded forever.
70 He chose his servant David,
and took him from the sheepfolds;
71 from tending the nursing ewes he brought him
to be the shepherd of his people Jacob,
of Israel, his inheritance.
72 With upright heart he tended them,
and guided them with skillful hand.

Psalm 79

A Psalm of Asaph.

O God, the nations have come
into your inheritance;
they have defiled your holy temple;
they have laid Jerusalem in ruins.
2 They have given the bodies of your servants
to the birds of the air for food,
the flesh of your faithful to the
wild animals of the earth.
3 They have poured out their blood like water
all around Jerusalem,
and there was no one to bury them.
4 We have become a taunt to our neighbors,

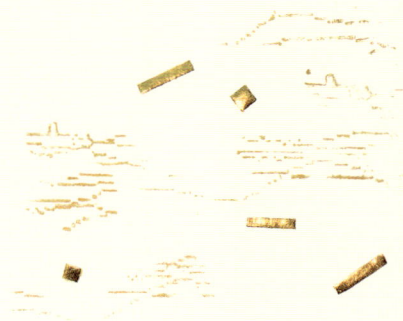

mocked and derided by those around us.

5 How long, O LORD? Will you be angry forever?
    Will your jealous wrath burn like fire?
6 Pour out your anger on the nations
    that do not know you,
  and on the kingdoms
    that do not call on your name.
7 For they have devoured Jacob
    and laid waste his habitation.

8 Do not remember against us the iniquities
        of our ancestors;
    let your compassion come speedily
        to meet us,
    for we are brought very low.
9 Help us, O God of our salvation,
        for the glory of your name;
    deliver us, and forgive our sins,
        for your name's sake.
10 Why should the nations say,
        "Where is their God?"
    Let the avenging of the outpoured
        blood of your servants
    be known among the nations before our eyes.

11 Let the groans of the prisoners
        come before you;
    according to your great power preserve
        those doomed to die.
12 Return sevenfold into the bosom
        of our neighbors
    the taunts with which they taunted you,
        O Lord!
13 Then we your people, the flock
        of your pasture,
    will give thanks to you forever;
    from generation to generation we will
        recount your praise.

Psalm 80

(To the leader: on Lilies, a Covenant. Of Asaph. A Psalm.)

Give ear, O Shepherd of Israel,
    you who lead Joseph like a flock!
You who are enthroned upon the cherubim,
    shine forth
2   before Ephraim and Benjamin and Manasseh.
Stir up your might,
    and come to save us!

3 Restore us, O God;
    let your face shine, that we may be saved.

ʲ Syr: Heb strife
*ᵏ Heb adds from verse 17
and upon the one whom
you made strong for
yourself*
ˡ Cn: Heb it is cut down

*j Lament
vi Liturgy*

4 O LORD God of hosts,
    how long will you be angry with your
        people's prayers?
5 You have fed them with the bread of tears,
    and given them tears to drink
        in full measure.
6 You make us the scorn of our neighbors;
    our enemies laugh among themselves.

7 Restore us, O God of hosts;
    let your face shine, that we may be saved.

8 You brought a vine out of Egypt;
    you drove out the nations and planted it.
9 You cleared the ground for it;
    it took deep root and filled the land.
10 The mountains were covered with its shade,
    the mighty cedars with its branches;
11 it sent out its branches to the sea,
    and its shoots to the River.
12 Why then have you broken down its walls,
    so that all who pass along the way
        pluck its fruit?
13 The boar from the forest ravages it,
    and all that move in the field feed on it.

14 Turn again, O God of hosts;
    look down from heaven, and see;
    have regard for this vine,
15   the stock that your right hand planted.
16 They have burned it with fire,
        they have cut it down;
    may they perish at the rebuke
        of your countenance.
17 But let your hand be upon the one
        at your right hand,
    the one whom you made strong for yourself.
18 Then we will never turn back from you;
    give us life, and we will call on your name.

19 Restore us, O LORD God of hosts;
    let your face shine, that we may be saved.

Psalm 81

(To the leader: according to The Gittith. Of Asaph.)

Sing aloud to God our strength;
    shout for joy to the God of Jacob.
2 Raise a song, sound the tambourine,
    the sweet lyre with the harp.
3 Blow the trumpet at the new moon,
    at the full moon, on our festal day.
4 For it is a statute for Israel,

an ordinance of the God of Jacob.
5 He made it a decree in Joseph,
  when he went out over the land of Egypt.

I hear a voice I had not known :
6 "I relieved your shoulder of the burden;
  your hands were freed from the basket.
7 In distress you called, and I rescued you;
  I answered you in the secret
    place of thunder;
  I tested you at the waters of Meribah. Selah
8 Hear, O my people, while I admonish you :
  O Israel, if you would but listen to me !
9 There shall be no strange god among you;
  you shall not bow down to a foreign god.
10 I am the LORD your God,
  who brought you up out of the land of Egypt.
  Open your mouth wide and I will fill it.

11 "But my people did not listen to my voice;
  Israel would not submit to me.
12 So I gave them over to their stubborn hearts,
  to follow their own counsels.
13 O that my people would listen to me,
  that Israel would walk in my ways !
14 Then I would quickly subdue their enemies,
  and turn my hand against their foes.
15 Those who hate the LORD would
    cringe before him,
  and their doom would last forever.
16 I would feed you with the finest of the wheat,
  and with honey from the rock
    I would satisfy you."

VI Psalm 82

A Psalm of Asaph.

God has taken his place in the divine council;
  in the midst of the gods he holds judgment :
2 "How long will you judge unjustly
  and show partiality to the wicked? Selah
3 Give justice to the weak and the orphan;
  maintain the right of the lowly
    and the destitute.
4 Rescue the weak and the needy;
  deliver them from the hand of the wicked."

5 They have neither knowledge nor
    understanding,
  they walk around in darkness;
  all the foundations of the earth are shaken.

6 I say, "You are gods,
  children of the Most High, all of you;
7 nevertheless, you shall die like mortals,
  and fall like any prince."

8 Rise up, O God, judge the earth;
  for all the nations belong to you !

Psalm 83

A Song. A Psalm of Asaph.

O God, do not keep silence;
  do not hold your peace or be still, O God !
2 Even now your enemies are in tumult;
  those who hate you have raised their heads.
3 They lay crafty plans against your people;
  they consult together against
    those you protect.
4 They say, "Come, let us wipe them
    out as a nation;
  let the name of Israel be remembered
    no more."
5 They conspire with one accord;
  against you they make a covenant —
6 the tents of Edom and the Ishmaelites,
  Moab and the Hagrites,
7 Gebal and Ammon and Amalek,
  Philistia with the inhabitants of Tyre;
8 Assyria also has joined them;
  they are the strong arm of the
    children of Lot. Selah

9 Do to them as you did to Midian,
  as to Sisera and Jabin at the Wadi Kishon,
10 who were destroyed at En-dor,
  who became dung for the ground.
11 Make their nobles like Oreb and Zeeb,
  all their princes like Zebah and Zalmunna,
12 who said, "Let us take the pastures of God
  for our own possession."

13 O my God, make them like whirling dust,
  like chaff before the wind.
14 As fire consumes the forest,
  as the flame sets the mountains ablaze,
15 so pursue them with your tempest
  and terrify them with your hurricane.
16 Fill their faces with shame,
  so that they may seek your name, O LORD.
17 Let them be put to shame and
    dismayed forever;
  let them perish in disgrace.
18 Let them know that you alone,

h Or against
c Heb his
i Cn Compare verse 16 b;
  Heb he would feed him
j Or fall as one man,
  O princes
k Or a tumbleweed

VI Liturgy
I Lament

whose name is the LORD,
are the Most High over all the earth.

Psalm 84

To the leader: according to The Gittith. Of the Korahites.
A Psalm.

How lovely is your dwelling place,
O LORD of hosts!
2 My soul longs, indeed it faints
for the courts of the LORD;
my heart and my flesh sing for joy
to the living God.

3 Even the sparrow finds a home,
and the swallow a nest for herself,
where she may lay her young,
at your altars, O LORD of hosts,
my King and my God.
4 Happy are those who live in your house,
ever singing your praise.   *Selah*

5 Happy are those whose strength is in you,
in whose heart are the highways to Zion.
6 As they go through the valley of Baca
they make it a place of springs;
the early rain also covers it with pools.
7 They go from strength to strength;
the God of gods will be seen in Zion.

8 O LORD God of hosts, hear my prayer;
give ear, O God of Jacob!   *Selah*
9 Behold our shield, O God;
look on the face of your anointed.

10 For a day in your courts is better
than a thousand elsewhere.
I would rather be a doorkeeper in
the house of my God
than live in the tents of wickedness.
11 For the LORD God is a sun and shield:
he bestows favor and honor.
No good thing does the LORD withhold
from those who walk uprightly.
12 O LORD of hosts,
happy is everyone who trusts in you.

Heb lacks to Zion
Gk: Heb but let them not
turn back to folly

VIII Zion Songs
1 Lament

Psalm 85

To the leader. Of the Korahites. A Psalm.

LORD, you were favorable to your land;
you restored the fortunes of Jacob.
2 You forgave the iniquity of your people;
you pardoned all their sin.   *Selah*
3 You withdrew all your wrath;
you turned from your hot anger.

4 Restore us again, O God of our salvation,
and put away your indignation toward us.
5 Will you be angry with us forever?
Will you prolong your anger
to all generations?
6 Will you not revive us again,
so that your people may rejoice in you?
7 Show us your steadfast love, O LORD,
and grant us your salvation.

8 Let me hear what God the LORD will speak,
for he will speak peace to his people,
to his faithful, to those who turn to
him in their hearts.
9 Surely his salvation is at hand for
those who fear him,
that his glory may dwell in our land.

10 Steadfast love and faithfulness will meet;
righteousness and peace will kiss each other.
11 Faithfulness will spring up from the ground,
and righteousness will look down
from the sky.
12 The LORD will give what is good,
and our land will yield its increase.
13 Righteousness will go before him,
and will make a path for his steps.

Psalm 86

A Prayer of David.

Incline your ear, O LORD, and answer me,
for I am poor and needy.
2 Preserve my life, for I am devoted to you;
save your servant who trusts in you.
You are my God; 3 be gracious to me, O Lord,
for to you do I cry all day long.
4 Gladden the soul of your servant,
for to you, O Lord, I lift up my soul.
5 For you, O Lord, are good and forgiving,
abounding in steadfast love to all
who call on you.
6 Give ear, O LORD, to my prayer;

listen to my cry of supplication.

7 In the day of my trouble I call on you,
  for you will answer me.

8 There is none like you among the gods, O Lord,
  nor are there any works like yours.
9 All the nations you have made shall come
  and bow down before you, O Lord,
  And shall glorify your name.
10 For you are great and do wondrous things;
  you alone are God.
11 Teach me your way, O LORD,
  that I may walk in your truth;
  give me an undivided heart to
    revere your name.
12 I give thanks to you, O Lord my God,
  with my whole heart,
  And I will glorify your name forever.
13 For great is your steadfast love toward me;
  you have delivered my soul from
    the depths of Sheol.

14 O God, the insolent rise up against me;
  a band of ruffians seeks my life,
  And they do not set you before them.
15 But you, O Lord, are a God
    merciful and gracious,
    slow to anger and abounding in steadfast
    love and faithfulness.
16 Turn to me and be gracious to me;
  give your strength to your servant;
  save the child of your serving girl.
17 Show me a sign of your favor,
  so that those who hate me may see it
    and be put to shame,
  because you, LORD, have helped me
    and comforted me.

Psalm 87

Of the Korahites. A Psalm. A Song.

On the holy mount stands the city he founded;
2 the LORD loves the gates of Zion
  more than all the dwellings of Jacob.
3 Glorious things are spoken of you,
  O city of God.   *Selah*

4 Among those who know me I mention
    Rahab and Babylon;
  Philistia too, and Tyre, with Ethiopia —
  "This one was born there," they say.

5 And of Zion it shall be said,
  "This one and that one were born in it";
  for the Most High himself will establish it.
6 The LORD records, as he registers the peoples,
  "This one was born there."   *Selah*

7 Singers and dancers alike say,
  "All my springs are in you."

Psalm 88

*A Song. A Psalm of the Korahites. To the leader:
according to Mahalath Leannoth. A Maskil of
Heman the Ezrahite.*

O LORD, God of my salvation,
  when, at night, I cry out in your presence,
2 let my prayer come before you;
  incline your ear to my cry.

3 For my soul is full of troubles,
  and my life draws near to Sheol.
4 I am counted among those who go
    down to the Pit;
  I am like those who have no help,
5 like those forsaken among the dead,
  like the slain that lie in the grave,
  like those whom you remember no more,
  for they are cut off from your hand.
6 You have put me in the depths of the Pit,
  in the regions dark and deep.
7 Your wrath lies heavy upon me,
  and you overwhelm me with
    all your waves.   *Selah*

8 You have caused my companions to shun me;
  you have made me a thing of horror to them.
  I am shut in so that I cannot escape;
9 my eye grows dim through sorrow.
  Every day I call on you, O LORD;
  I spread out my hands to you.
10 Do you work wonders for the dead?
  Do the shades rise up to praise you?   *Selah*
11 Is your steadfast love declared in the grave,
  or your faithfulness in Abaddon?
12 Are your wonders known in the darkness,
  or your saving help in the land
    of forgetfulness?

13 But I, O LORD, cry out to you;
  in the morning my prayer comes before you.
14 O LORD, why do you cast me off?
  Why do you hide your face from me?
15 Wretched and close to death
    from my youth up,

RSB
Psalm 88:15

v Or Nubia; Heb Cush

VIII Zion Songs
i Lament

I suffer your terrors; I am desperate.

16 Your wrath has swept over me;
   your dread assaults destroy me.

17 They surround me like a flood all day long;
   from all sides they close in on me.

18 You have caused friend and neighbor
   to shun me;
   my companions are in darkness.

Psalm 89

A Maskil of Ethan the Ezrahite.

I will sing of your steadfast love,
   O LORD, forever;
   with my mouth I will proclaim your
   faithfulness to all generations.

2 I declare that your steadfast love
   is established forever;
   your faithfulness is as firm as the heavens.

3 You said, "I have made a covenant
   with my chosen one,
   I have sworn to my servant David:

4 'I will establish your descendants forever,
   and build your throne for
   all generations.'"   Selah

5 Let the heavens praise your wonders, O LORD,
   your faithfulness in the assembly
   of the holy ones.

6 For who in the skies can be compared
   to the LORD?
   Who among the heavenly beings
   is like the LORD,

7 a God feared in the council of the holy ones,
   great and awesome above all that
   are around him?

8 O LORD God of hosts,
   who is as mighty as you, O LORD?
   Your faithfulness surrounds you.

9 You rule the raging of the sea;
   when its waves rise, you still them.

10 You crushed Rahab like a carcass;
   you scattered your enemies with
   your mighty arm.

11 The heavens are yours, the earth also is yours;
   the world and all that is in it —you have
   founded them.

12 The north and the south —you created them;
   Tabor and Hermon joyously
   praise your name.

13 You have a mighty arm;
   strong is your hand, high your right hand.

14 Righteousness and justice are the foundation
   of your throne;
   steadfast love and faithfulness go before you.

15 Happy are the people who know
   the festal shout,
   who walk, O LORD, in the light of
   your countenance;

16 they exult in your name all day long,
   and extol your righteousness.

17 For you are the glory of their strength;
   by your favor our horn is exalted.

18 For our shield belongs to the LORD,
   our king to the Holy One of Israel.

19 Then you spoke in a vision to your
   faithful one, and said:
   "I have set the crown on one who is mighty,
   I have exalted one chosen from the people.

20 I have found my servant David;
   with my holy oil I have anointed him;

21 my hand shall always remain with him;
   my arm also shall strengthen him.

22 The enemy shall not outwit him,
   the wicked shall not humble him.

23 I will crush his foes before him
   and strike down those who hate him.

24 My faithfulness and steadfast love
   shall be with him;
   and in my name his horn shall be exalted.

25 I will set his hand on the sea
   and his right hand on the rivers.

26 He shall cry to me, 'You are my Father,
   my God, and the Rock of my salvation!'

27 I will make him the firstborn,
   the highest of the kings of the earth.

28 Forever I will keep my steadfast love for him,
   and my covenant with him will stand firm.

29 I will establish his line forever,
   and his throne as long as the heavens endure.

30 If his children forsake my law
   and do not walk according to my ordinances,

31 if they violate my statutes
   and do not keep my commandments,

32 then I will punish their transgression
   with the rod
   and their iniquity with scourges;

33 but I will not remove from him
   my steadfast love,
   or be false to my faithfulness.

34 I will not violate my covenant,
   or alter the word that went forth
   from my lips.

35 Once and for all I have sworn by my holiness;
   I will not lie to David.

w Meaning of Heb uncertain
x Gk: Heb the steadfast
   love of the LORD
y Gk: Syr Heb greatly
   awesome
z Or Zaphon and Yamin
a Cn: Heb are exalted in
b Cn: Heb help
c Cn: Heb removed his
   cleanness
d Meaning of Heb uncertain
e Cn: Heb bosom all of
   many peoples

VII Royal

³⁶ His line shall continue forever,
   and his throne endure before me
      like the sun.
³⁷ It shall be established forever like the moon,
   an enduring witness in the skies."   Selah

³⁸ But now you have spurned and rejected him;
   you are full of wrath against your anointed.
³⁹ You have renounced the covenant
      with your servant:
   you have defiled his crown in the dust.
⁴⁰ You have broken through all his walls;
   you have laid his strongholds in ruins.
⁴¹ All who pass by plunder him;
   he has become the scorn of his neighbors.
⁴² You have exalted the right hand of his foes;
   you have made all his enemies rejoice.
⁴³ Moreover, you have turned back
      the edge of his sword,
   and you have not supported him in battle.
⁴⁴ You have removed the scepter from his hand,
   and hurled his throne to the ground.
⁴⁵ You have cut short the days of his youth;
   you have covered him with shame.   Selah

⁴⁶ How long, O LORD? Will you hide
      yourself forever?
   How long will your wrath burn like fire?
⁴⁷ Remember how short my time is—
   for what vanity you have created all mortals!
⁴⁸ Who can live and never see death?
   Who can escape the power of Sheol?   Selah

⁴⁹ Lord, where is your steadfast love of old,
   which by your faithfulness
      you swore to David?
⁵⁰ Remember, O Lord, how your
      servant is taunted;
   how I bear in my bosom the
      insults of the peoples,
⁵¹ with which your enemies taunt, O LORD,
   with which they taunted the footsteps
      of your anointed.

⁵² Blessed be the LORD forever.
   Amen & Amen

BOOK IV

Psalm 90

A Prayer of Moses, the man of God.

Lord, you have been our dwelling place
  in all generations.
2 Before the mountains were brought forth,
  or ever you had formed the
    earth and the world,
  from everlasting to everlasting you are God.

3 You turn us back to dust,
  and say, "Turn back, you mortals."
4 For a thousand years in your sight
  are like yesterday when it is past,
  or like a watch in the night.

5 You sweep them away; they are like a dream,
  like grass that is renewed in the morning:
6 in the morning it flourishes and is renewed;
  in the evening it fades and withers.

7 For we are consumed by your anger;
  by your wrath we are overwhelmed.
8 You have set our iniquities before you,
  our secret sins in the light of
    your countenance.

9 For all our days pass away under your wrath;
  our years come to an end like a sigh.
10 The days of our life are seventy years,
  or perhaps eighty, if we are strong;
  even then their span is only toil and trouble;
  they are soon gone, and we fly away.

11 Who considers the power of your anger?
  Your wrath is as great as the
    fear that is due you.
12 So teach us to count our days
  that we may gain a wise heart.

13 Turn, O LORD! How long?
  Have compassion on your servants!
14 Satisfy us in the morning with
    your steadfast love,
  so that we may rejoice and be
    glad all our days.
15 Make us glad as many days as you
    have afflicted us,
  and as many years as we have seen evil.
16 Let your work be manifest to your servants,
  and your glorious power to their children.
17 Let the favor of the Lord our God be upon us,
  and prosper for us the work of our hands—
  O prosper the work of our hands!

Psalm 91

You who live in the shelter of the Most High,
  who abide in the shadow of the Almighty,
2 will say to the LORD, "My refuge
    and my fortress;
  my God, in whom I trust."
3 For he will deliver you from the
    snare of the fowler
  and from the deadly pestilence;
4 he will cover you with his pinions,
  and under his wings you will find refuge;
  his faithfulness is a shield and buckler.
5 You will not fear the terror of the night,
  or the arrow that flies by day,
6 or the pestilence that stalks in darkness,
  or the destruction that wastes at noonday.

7 A thousand may fall at your side,
  ten thousand at your right hand,
  but it will not come near you.
8 You will only look with your eyes
  and see the punishment of the wicked.

9 Because you have made the LORD your refuge,
  the Most High your dwelling place,
10 no evil shall befall you,
  no scourge come near your tent.

11 For he will command his angels concerning you
  to guard you in all your ways.
12 On their hands they will bear you up,
  so that you will not dash your
    foot against a stone.
13 You will tread on the lion and the adder,
  the young lion and the serpent you will
    trample under foot.

14 Those who love me, I will deliver;
  I will protect those who know my name.
15 When they call to me, I will answer them;
  I will be with them in trouble,
  I will rescue them and honor them.
16 With long life I will satisfy them,
  and show them my salvation.

Psalm 92

A Psalm. A Song for the Sabbath Day.

It is good to give thanks to the LORD,
  to sing praises to your name, O Most High;
2 to declare your steadfast love in the morning,
  and your faithfulness by night,

3 to the music of the lute and the harp,
  to the melody of the lyre.
4 For you, O LORD, have made me
    glad by your work;
  at the works of your hands I sing for joy.

5 How great are your works, O LORD!
  Your thoughts are very deep!
6 The dullard cannot know,
  the stupid cannot understand this:
7 though the wicked sprout like grass
  and all evildoers flourish,
  they are doomed to destruction forever,
8 but you, O LORD, are on high forever.
9 For your enemies, O LORD,
  for your enemies shall perish;
  all evildoers shall be scattered.

10 But you have exalted my horn like
    that of the wild ox;
  you have poured over me fresh oil.
11 My eyes have seen the downfall of my enemies;
  my ears have heard the doom
    of my evil assailants.

12 The righteous flourish like the palm tree,
  and grow like a cedar in Lebanon.
13 They are planted in the house of the LORD;
  they flourish in the courts of our God.
14 In old age they still produce fruit;
  they are always green and full of sap,
15 showing that the LORD is upright;
  he is my rock, and there is no
    unrighteousness in him.

Psalm 93

The LORD is king, he is robed in majesty;
  the LORD is robed, he is girded with strength.
He has established the world;
    it shall never be moved;
2 your throne is established from of old;
  you are from everlasting.

3 The floods have lifted up, O LORD,
  the floods have lifted up their voice;
  the floods lift up their roaring.
4 More majestic than the thunders
    of mighty waters,
  more majestic than the waves of the sea,
  majestic on high is the LORD!

j Another reading is *our
  refuge*
g Heb *humankind*
h Syr: Heb *we bring our
  years to an end*
i Cn Compare Gk Syr
  Jerome Tg: Heb *pride*
j Traditional rendering of
  Heb *Shaddai*
k Cn: Heb *Because you,
  LORD, are my refuge;
  you have made*
l Syr: Meaning of Heb
  uncertain
m Cn: Heb *majestic are
  the waves*

I Lament
IV Confidence
II Hymn

⁵ Your decrees are very sure;
   holiness befits your house,
   O LORD, forevermore.

Psalm 94

O LORD, you God of vengeance,
   you God of vengeance, shine forth!
² Rise up, O judge of the earth;
   give to the proud what they deserve!
³ O LORD, how long shall the wicked,
   how long shall the wicked exult?

⁴ They pour out their arrogant words;
   all the evildoers boast.
⁵ They crush your people, O LORD,
   and afflict your heritage.
⁶ They kill the widow and the stranger,
   they murder the orphan,
⁷ and they say, "The LORD does not see;
   the God of Jacob does not perceive."

⁸ Understand, O dullest of the people;
   fools, when will you be wise?
⁹ He who planted the ear, does he not hear?
   He who formed the eye, does he not see?
¹⁰ He who disciplines the nations,
   he who teaches knowledge to humankind,
   does he not chastise?
¹¹ The LORD knows our thoughts,[n]
   that they are but an empty breath.

¹² Happy are those whom you discipline, O LORD,
   and whom you teach out of your law,
¹³ giving them respite from days of trouble,
   until a pit is dug for the wicked.
¹⁴ For the LORD will not forsake his people;
   he will not abandon his heritage;
¹⁵ for justice will return to the righteous,
   and all the upright in heart will follow it.

¹⁶ Who rises up for me against the wicked?
   Who stands up for me against evildoers?
¹⁷ If the LORD had not been my help,
   my soul would soon have lived
   in the land of silence.
¹⁸ When I thought, "My foot is slipping,"
   your steadfast love, O LORD, held me up.
¹⁹ When the cares of my heart are many,
   your consolations cheer my soul.
²⁰ Can wicked rulers be allied with you,
   those who contrive mischief by statute?
²¹ They band together against the

life of the righteous,
   and condemn the innocent to death.
²² But the LORD has become my stronghold,
   and my God the rock of my refuge.
²³ He will repay them for their iniquity
   and wipe them out for their wickedness;
   the LORD our God will wipe them out.

Psalm 95

O come, let us sing to the LORD;
   let us make a joyful noise to the
   rock of our salvation!
² Let us come into his presence with
   thanksgiving;
   let us make a joyful noise to him
   with songs of praise!
³ For the LORD is a great God,
   and a great King above all gods.
⁴ In his hand are the depths of the earth;
   the heights of the mountains are his also.
⁵ The sea is his, for he made it,
   and the dry land, which his
   hands have formed.

⁶ O come, let us worship and bow down,
   let us kneel before the LORD, our Maker!
⁷ For he is our God,
   and we are the people of his pasture,
   and the sheep of his hand.

O that today you would listen to his voice!
⁸ Do not harden your hearts, as at Meribah,
   as on the day at Massah in the wilderness,
⁹ when your ancestors tested me,
   and put me to the proof, though
   they had seen my work.
¹⁰ For forty years I loathed that generation
   and said, "They are a people whose
   hearts go astray,
   and they do not regard my ways."
¹¹ Therefore in my anger I swore,
   "They shall not enter my rest."

Psalm 96

O sing to the LORD a new song;
   sing to the LORD, all the earth.
² Sing to the LORD, bless his name;
   tell of his salvation from day to day.
³ Declare his glory among the nations,
   his marvelous works among all the peoples.

RSB
Psalm 95:7-8

ⁿ Heb *the thoughts of humankind*

l Lament
ll Hymn

4 For great is the LORD, and greatly to be praised:
    he is to be revered above all gods.
5 For all the gods of the peoples are idols,
    but the LORD made the heavens.
6 Honor and majesty are before him :
    strength and beauty are in his sanctuary.

7 Ascribe to the LORD, O families of the peoples,
    ascribe to the LORD glory and strength.
8 Ascribe to the LORD the glory due his name :
    bring an offering, and come into his courts.
9 Worship the LORD in holy splendor:
    tremble before him, all the earth!

10 Say among the nations,"The LORD is king!
    The world is firmly established :
      it shall never be moved.
    He will judge the peoples with equity."
11 Let the heavens be glad, and let
      the earth rejoice;
    let the sea roar, and all that fills it;
12 let the field exult, and everything in it.
    Then shall all the trees of the forest sing for joy
13 before the LORD; for he is coming,
    for he is coming to judge the earth.
    He will judge the world with righteousness,
      and the peoples with his truth.

Psalm 97

1 The LORD is king! Let the earth rejoice;
    let the many coastlands be glad !
2 Clouds and thick darkness are all around him;
    righteousness and justice are the
      foundation of his throne.
3 Fire goes before him,
    and consumes his adversaries on every side.
4 His lightnings light up the world;
    the earth sees and trembles.
5 The mountains melt like wax before the LORD,
    before the LORD of all the earth.

6 The heavens proclaim his righteousness;
    and all the peoples behold his glory.
7 All worshipers of images are put to shame,
    those who make their boast
      in worthless idols;
    all gods bow down before him.
8 Zion hears and is glad,
    and the towns of Judah rejoice,
    because of your judgments, O God.
9 For you, O LORD, are most high
      over all the earth;

you are exalted far above all gods.

10 The LORD loves those who hate evil;
    he guards the lives of his faithful;
    he rescues them from the
      hand of the wicked.
11 Light dawns for the righteous,
    and joy for the upright in heart.
12 Rejoice in the LORD, O you righteous,
    and give thanks to his holy name !

Psalm 98

A Psalm.

1 O sing to the LORD a new song,
    for he has done marvelous things.
    His right hand and his holy arm
      have gotten him victory.
2 The LORD has made known his victory;
    he has revealed his vindication
      in the sight of the nations.
3 He has remembered his steadfast
      love and faithfulness
    to the house of Israel.
    All the ends of the earth have seen
      the victory of our God.

4 Make a joyful noise to the LORD, all the earth;
    break forth into joyous song and sing praises.
5 Sing praises to the LORD with the lyre,
    with the lyre and the sound of melody.
6 With trumpets and the sound of the horn
    make a joyful noise before the
      King, the LORD.

7 Let the sea roar, and all that fills it;
    the world and those who live in it.
8 Let the floods clap their hands;
    let the hills sing together for joy
9 at the presence of the LORD, for he is coming
    to judge the earth.
    He will judge the world with righteousness,
    and the peoples with equity.

Psalm 99

1 The LORD is king; let the peoples tremble !
    He sits enthroned upon the cherubim;
      let the earth quake !
2 The LORD is great in Zion;
    he is exalted over all the peoples.
3 Let them praise your great and awesome name.

g Heb daughters
f Cn : Heb you who love the
    Lord hate
g Gk Syr Jerome : Heb
    is seven

h Hymn

Holy is he!
4 Mighty King, lover of justice,
    you have established equity;
you have executed justice
    and righteousness in Jacob.
5 Extol the LORD our God;
    worship at his footstool.
    Holy is he!

6 Moses and Aaron were among his priests,
    Samuel also was among those
        who called on his name.
    They cried to the LORD, and
        he answered them.
7 He spoke to them in the pillar of cloud;
    they kept his decrees,
        and the statutes that he gave them.

8 O LORD our God, you answered them;
    you were a forgiving God to them,
    but an avenger of their wrongdoings.
    Extol the LORD our God,
        and worship at his holy mountain;
        for the LORD our God is holy.

Psalm 100

A Psalm of thanksgiving.

Make a joyful noise to the LORD, all the earth.
2   Worship the LORD with gladness;
        come into his presence with singing.

3   Know that the LORD is God.
        It is he that made us, and we are his;
        we are his people, and the sheep
            of his pasture.

4   Enter his gates with thanksgiving,
        and his courts with praise.
        Give thanks to him, bless his name.

5   For the LORD is good;
        his steadfast love endures forever,
        and his faithfulness to all generations.

Psalm 101

Of David. A Psalm.

I will sing of loyalty and justice;
    to you, O LORD, I will sing.
2 I will study the way that is blameless.
    When shall I attain it?

I will walk with integrity of heart
        within my house;
3 I will not set before my eyes
        anything that is base.

I hate the work of those who fall away;
        it shall not cling to me.
4 Perverseness of heart shall be far from me;
        I will know nothing of evil.

5 One who secretly slanders a neighbor
        I will destroy.
    A haughty look and an arrogant heart
        I will not tolerate.

6 I will look with favor on the
        faithful in the land,
    so that they may live with me;
    whoever walks in the way that is blameless
        shall minister to me.

7 No one who practices deceit
        shall remain in my house;
    no one who utters lies
        shall continue in my presence.

8 Morning by morning I will destroy
        all the wicked in the land,
    cutting off all evildoers
        from the city of the LORD.

Psalm 102

A prayer of one afflicted, when faint and
    pleading before the LORD.

Hear my prayer, O LORD;
let my cry come to you.

2 Do not hide your face from me
        in the day of my distress.
    Incline your ear to me;
        answer me speedily in the day when I call.

3 For my days pass away like smoke,
        and my bones burn like a furnace.
4 My heart is stricken & withered like grass;
        I am too wasted to eat my bread.
5 Because of my loud groaning
        my bones cling to my skin.
6 I am like an owl of the wilderness,
        like a little owl of the waste places.
7 I lie awake;

I am like a lonely bird on the housetop.
8 All day long my enemies taunt me;
    those who deride me use my
        name for a curse.
9 For I eat ashes like bread,
    and mingle tears with my drink,
10 because of your indignation and anger;
    for you have lifted me up
        and thrown me aside.
11 My days are like an evening shadow;
    I wither away like grass.

12 But you, O LORD, are enthroned forever;
    your name endures to all generations.
13 You will rise up & have compassion on Zion,
    for it is time to favor it;
        the appointed time has come.
14 For your servants hold its stones dear,
    and have pity on its dust.
15 The nations will fear the name of the LORD,
    and all the kings of the earth your glory.
16 For the LORD will build up Zion;
    he will appear in his glory.
17 He will regard the prayer of the destitute,
    and will not despise their prayer.

18 Let this be recorded for a generation to come,
    so that a people yet unborn may
        praise the LORD:
19 that he looked down from his holy height,
    from heaven the LORD looked at the earth,
20 to hear the groans of the prisoners,
    to set free those who were doomed to die;
21 so that the name of the LORD may
        be declared in Zion,
    and his praise in Jerusalem,
22 when peoples gather together,
    and kingdoms, to worship the LORD.

23 He has broken my strength in midcourse;
    he has shortened my days.
24 "O my God," I say, "do not take me away
    at the midpoint of my life,
    you whose years endure
        throughout all generations."

25 Long ago you laid the foundation of the earth,
    and the heavens are the work of your hands.
26 They will perish, but you endure;
    they will all wear out like a garment.
    You change them like clothing,
        and they pass away;
27   but you are the same, and your
        years have no end.

28 The children of your servants shall live secure;
    their offspring shall be established
        in your presence.

Psalm 103

Of David.

Bless the LORD, O my soul,
    and all that is within me,
    bless his holy name.
2 Bless the LORD, O my soul,
    and do not forget all his benefits —
3 who forgives all your iniquity,
    who heals all your diseases,
4 who redeems your life from the Pit,
    who crowns you with steadfast
        love and mercy,
5 who satisfies you with good as long as you live
    so that your youth is renewed like the eagle's.

6 The LORD works vindication
    and justice for all who are oppressed.
7 He made known his ways to Moses,
    his acts to the people of Israel.
8 The LORD is merciful and gracious,
    slow to anger and abounding
        in steadfast love.
9 He will not always accuse,
    nor will he keep his anger forever.
10 He does not deal with us according to our sins,
    nor repay us according to our iniquities.
11 For as the heavens are high above the earth,
    so great is his steadfast love toward
        those who fear him;
12 as far as the east is from the west,
    so far he removes our transgressions from us.
13 As a father has compassion for his children,
    so the LORD has compassion for
        those who fear him.
14 For he knows how we were made;
    he remembers that we are dust.

15 As for mortals, their days are like grass;
    they flourish like a flower of the field;
16 for the wind passes over it, and it is gone,
    and its place knows it no more.
17 But the steadfast love of the LORD is from
        everlasting to everlasting
    on those who fear him,
    and his righteousness to children's children,
18 to those who keep his covenant
    and remember to do his commandments.

† Meaning of Heb uncertain

11 Hymn

¹⁹ The LORD has established his throne
in the heavens,
and his kingdom rules over all.
²⁰ Bless the LORD, O you his angels,
you mighty ones who do his bidding,
obedient to his spoken word.
²¹ Bless the LORD, all his hosts,
his ministers that do his will.
²² Bless the LORD, all his works,
in all places of his dominion.
Bless the LORD, O my soul.

Psalm 104

Bless the LORD, O my soul.
O LORD my God, you are very great.
You are clothed with honor and majesty,
² wrapped in light as with a garment.
You stretch out the heavens like a tent,
³ you set the beams of your chambers
on the waters,
you make the clouds your chariot,
you ride on the wings of the wind.
⁴ you make the winds your messengers,
fire and flame your ministers.

⁵ You set the earth on its foundations,
so that it shall never be shaken.
⁶ You cover it with the deep as with a garment;
the waters stood above the mountains.
⁷ At your rebuke they flee;
at the sound of your thunder
they take to flight.
⁸ They rose up to the mountains,
ran down to the valleys
to the place that you appointed for them.
⁹ You set a boundary that they may not pass,
so that they might not again cover the earth.

¹⁰ You make springs gush forth in the valleys;
they flow between the hills,
¹¹ giving drink to every wild animal;
the wild asses quench their thirst.
¹² By the streams the birds of the air
have their habitation;
they sing among the branches.
¹³ From your lofty abode you water
the mountains;
the earth is satisfied with the
fruit of your work.

¹⁴ You cause the grass to grow for the cattle,
and plants for people to use,

to bring forth food from the earth,
¹⁵ and wine to gladden the human heart,
oil to make the face shine,
and bread to strengthen the human heart.
¹⁶ The trees of the LORD are watered abundantly,
the cedars of Lebanon that he planted.
¹⁷ In them the birds build their nests;
the stork has its home in the fir trees.
¹⁸ The high mountains are for the wild goats;
the rocks are a refuge for the coneys.
¹⁹ You have made the moon to mark the seasons;
the sun knows its time for setting.
²⁰ You make darkness, & it is night,
when all the animals of the forest
come creeping out.
²¹ The young lions roar for their prey,
seeking their food from God.
²² When the sun rises, they withdraw
and lie down in their dens.
²³ People go out to their work
and to their labor until the evening.

²⁴ O LORD, how manifold are your works!
In wisdom you have made them all;
the earth is full of your creatures.
²⁵ Yonder is the sea, great and wide,
creeping things innumerable are there,
living things both small and great.
²⁶ There go the ships,
and Leviathan that you formed to sport in it.

²⁷ These all look to you
to give them their food in due season;
²⁸ when you give to them, they gather it up;
when you open your hand, they are
filled with good things.
²⁹ When you hide your face, they are dismayed;
when you take away their breath, they die
and return to their dust.
³⁰ When you send forth your spirit,
they are created;
and you renew the face of the ground.

³¹ May the glory of the LORD endure forever;
may the LORD rejoice in his works—
³² who looks on the earth and it trembles,
who touches the mountains and they smoke.
³³ I will sing to the LORD as long as I live;
I will sing praise to my God
while I have being.
³⁴ May my meditation be pleasing to him,
for I rejoice in the LORD.
Let sinners be consumed from the earth,
³⁵ and let the wicked be no more.

u,v,w,x
Heb *his*
Heb *By them*
Or *to cultivate*
Or *your breath*

ll Hymn

Bless the LORD, O my soul.
Praise the LORD!

Psalm 105

O give thanks to the LORD, call on his name,
  make known his deeds among the peoples.

2 Sing to him, sing praises to him;
  tell of all his wonderful works.

3 Glory in his holy name;
  let the hearts of those who seek
    the LORD rejoice.

4 Seek the LORD and his strength;
  seek his presence continually.

5 Remember the wonderful works he has done,
  his miracles, and the judgments
    he has uttered.

6 O offspring of his servant Abraham,
  children of Jacob, his chosen ones.

7 He is the LORD our God;
  his judgments are in all the earth.

8 He is mindful of his covenant forever,
  of the word that he commanded, for a
    thousand generations,

9 the covenant that he made with Abraham,
  his sworn promise to Isaac,

10 which he confirmed to Jacob as a statute,
  to Israel as an everlasting covenant,

11 saying, "To you I will give the land of Canaan
  as your portion for an inheritance."

12 When they were few in number,
  of little account, and strangers in it,

13 wandering from nation to nation,
  from one kingdom to another people,

14 he allowed no one to oppress them;
  he rebuked kings on their account,

15 saying, "Do not touch my anointed ones;
  do my prophets no harm."

16 When he summoned famine against the land,
  and broke every staff of bread,

17 he had sent a man ahead of them,
  Joseph, who was sold as a slave.

18 His feet were hurt with fetters,
  his neck was put in a collar of iron;

19 until what he had said came to pass,
  the word of the LORD kept testing him.

20 The king sent and released him;
  the ruler of the peoples set him free.

21 He made him lord of his house,
  and ruler of all his possessions,

22 to instruct his officials at his pleasure,
  and to teach his elders wisdom.

23 Then Israel came to Egypt;
  Jacob lived as an alien in the land of Ham.

24 And the LORD made his people very fruitful,
  and made them stronger than their foes,

25 whose hearts he then turned
    to hate his people,
  to deal craftily with his servants.

26 He sent his servant Moses,
  and Aaron whom he had chosen.

27 They performed his signs among them,
  and miracles in the land of Ham.

28 He sent darkness, and made the land dark;
  they rebelled against his words.

29 He turned their waters into blood,
  and caused their fish to die.

30 Their land swarmed with frogs,
  even in the chambers of their kings.

31 He spoke, and there came swarms of flies,
  and gnats throughout their country.

32 He gave them hail for rain,
  and lightning that flashed
    through their land.

33 He struck their vines and fig trees,
  and shattered the trees of their country.

34 He spoke, and the locusts came,
  and young locusts without number;

35 they devoured all the vegetation in their land,
  and ate up the fruit of their ground.

36 He struck down all the firstborn in their land,
  the first issue of all their strength.

37 Then he brought Israel out with
    silver and gold,
  and there was no one among their
    tribes who stumbled.

38 Egypt was glad when they departed,
  for dread of them had fallen upon it.

39 He spread a cloud for a covering,
  and fire to give light by night.

40 They asked, and he brought quails
  and gave them food from heaven
    in abundance.

41 He opened the rock, and water gushed out;
  it flowed through the desert like a river.

42 For he remembered his holy promise,
  and Abraham, his servant.

43 So he brought his people out with joy,
  his chosen ones with singing.

44 He gave them the lands of the nations,

b Another reading is Israel
  [compare 1 Chr 16.13]
c Gk Syr Jerome: Heb
  to bind
d Cn Compare Gk Syr: Heb
  They did not rebel
e Heb them

IX Historical

and they took possession of the
 wealth of the peoples,
⁴⁵ that they might keep his statutes
 and observe his laws.
 Praise the LORD!

Psalm 106

Praise the LORD!
 O give thanks to the LORD, for he is good;
  for his steadfast love endures forever.
² Who can utter the mighty doings of the LORD,
  or declare all his praise?
³ Happy are those who observe justice,
  who do righteousness at all times.

⁴ Remember me, O LORD, when you show
  favor to your people;
 help me when you deliver them;
⁵ that I may see the prosperity of
  your chosen ones,
 that I may rejoice in the gladness
  of your nation,
 that I may glory in your heritage.

⁶ Both we and our ancestors have sinned;
 we have committed iniquity,
  have done wickedly.
⁷ Our ancestors, when they were in Egypt,
 did not consider your wonderful works;
 they did not remember the abundance
  of your steadfast love,
 but rebelled against the Most High
  at the Red Sea.
⁸ Yet he saved them for his name's sake,
 so that he might make known
  his mighty power.
⁹ He rebuked the Red Sea, and it became dry;
 he led them through the deep as
  through a desert.
¹⁰ So he saved them from the hand of the foe,
 and delivered them from the
  hand of the enemy.
¹¹ The waters covered their adversaries;
 not one of them was left.
¹² Then they believed his words;
 they sang his praise.

¹³ But they soon forgot his works;
 they did not wait for his counsel.
¹⁴ But they had a wanton craving
 in the wilderness,
 and put God to the test in the desert;

¹⁵ he gave them what they asked,
 but sent a wasting disease among them.

¹⁶ They were jealous of Moses in the camp,
 and of Aaron, the holy one of the LORD.
¹⁷ The earth opened and swallowed up Dathan,
 and covered the faction of Abiram.
¹⁸ Fire also broke out in their company;
 the flame burned up the wicked.

¹⁹ They made a calf at Horeb
 and worshiped a cast image.
²⁰ They exchanged the glory of God
 for the image of an ox that eats grass.
²¹ They forgot God, their Savior,
 who had done great things in Egypt,
²² wondrous works in the land of Ham,
 and awesome deeds by the Red Sea.
²³ Therefore he said he would destroy them —
 had not Moses, his chosen one,
 stood in the breach before him,
 to turn away his wrath
  from destroying them.

²⁴ Then they despised the pleasant land,
 having no faith in his promise.
²⁵ They grumbled in their tents,
 and did not obey the voice of the LORD.
²⁶ Therefore he raised his hand
 and swore to them
 that he would make them fall
  in the wilderness,
²⁷ and would disperse their descendants
 among the nations,
 scattering them over the lands.

²⁸ Then they attached themselves to
 the Baal of Peor,
 and ate sacrifices offered to the dead;
²⁹ they provoked the LORD to anger
 with their deeds,
 and a plague broke out among them.
³⁰ Then Phinehas stood up and interceded,
 and the plague was stopped.
³¹ And that has been reckoned to
 him as righteousness
 from generation to generation forever.

³² They angered the LORD at the
 waters of Meribah,
 and it went ill with Moses on their account;
³³ for they made his spirit bitter,
 and he spoke words that were rash.

f Cn Compare 78.17, 56:
Heb rebelled at the sea
g·h·j
Or Sea of Reeds
i Compare Gk Mss: Heb
exchanged their glory
k Syr Compare Ezek 20:23:
Heb cause to fall
l Heb him

IX Historical

³⁴ They did not destroy the peoples,
      as the LORD commanded them,
³⁵ but they mingled with the nations
      and learned to do as they did.
³⁶ They served their idols,
      which became a snare to them.
³⁷ They sacrificed their sons
      and their daughters to the demons;
³⁸ they poured out innocent blood,
      the blood of their sons and daughters,
      whom they sacrificed to the idols of Canaan;
      and the land was polluted with blood.
³⁹ Thus they became unclean by their acts,
      and prostituted themselves in their doings.

⁴⁰ Then the anger of the LORD was kindled
            against his people,
      and he abhorred his heritage;
⁴¹ he gave them into the hand of the nations,
      so that those who hated them
            ruled over them.
⁴² Their enemies oppressed them,
      and they were brought into subjection
            under their power.
⁴³ Many times he delivered them,
      but they were rebellious in their purposes,
      and were brought low through their iniquity.
⁴⁴ Nevertheless he regarded their distress
      when he heard their cry.
⁴⁵ For their sake he remembered his covenant,
      & showed compassion according to the
            abundance of his steadfast love.
⁴⁶ He caused them to be pitied
      by all who held them captive.

⁴⁷ Save us, O LORD our God,
      and gather us from among the nations,
      that we may give thanks to your holy name
      and glory in your praise.

⁴⁸ Blessed be the LORD, the God of Israel,
      from everlasting to everlasting.
And let all the people say, "Amen."
      Praise the LORD!

Psalm 107

O give thanks to the LORD, for he is good;
 for his steadfast love endures forever.
2 Let the redeemed of the LORD say so,
 those he redeemed from trouble
3 and gathered in from the lands,
 from the east and from the west,
 from the north and from the south.

4 Some wandered in desert wastes,
 finding no way to an inhabited town;
5 hungry and thirsty,
 their soul fainted within them.
6 Then they cried to the LORD in their trouble,
 and he delivered them from their distress;
7 he led them by a straight way,
 until they reached an inhabited town.
8 Let them thank the LORD for his steadfast love,
 for his wonderful works to humankind.
9 For he satisfies the thirsty,
 and the hungry he fills with good things.

10 Some sat in darkness and in gloom,
 prisoners in misery and in irons,
11 for they had rebelled against the words of God,
 and spurned the counsel of the Most High.
12 Their hearts were bowed down
  with hard labor;
 they fell down, with no one to help.
13 Then they cried to the LORD in their trouble,
 and he saved them from their distress;
14 he brought them out of darkness and gloom,
 and broke their bonds asunder.
15 Let them thank the LORD for his steadfast love,
 for his wonderful works to humankind.
16 For he shatters the doors of bronze,
 and cuts in two the bars of iron.

17 Some were sick through their sinful ways,
 and because of their iniquities
  endured affliction;
18 they loathed any kind of food,
 and they drew near to the gates of death.
19 Then they cried to the LORD in their trouble,
 and he saved them from their distress;
20 he sent out his word and healed them,
 and delivered them from destruction.
21 Let them thank the LORD for his steadfast love,
 for his wonderful works to humankind.
22 And let them offer thanksgiving sacrifices,
 and tell of his deeds with songs of joy.

²³ Some went down to the sea in ships,
  doing business on the mighty waters;
²⁴ they saw the deeds of the LORD,
  his wondrous works in the deep.
²⁵ For he commanded and raised
   the stormy wind,
  which lifted up the waves of the sea.
²⁶ They mounted up to heaven, they went
   down to the depths;
  their courage melted away in their calamity;
²⁷ they reeled and staggered like drunkards,
  and were at their wits' end.
²⁸ Then they cried to the LORD in their trouble,
  and he brought them out from their distress;
²⁹ he made the storm be still,
  and the waves of the sea were hushed.
³⁰ Then they were glad because they had quiet,
  and he brought them to their desired haven.
³¹ Let them thank the LORD for his steadfast love,
  for his wonderful works to humankind.
³² Let them extol him in the congregation
   of the people,
  and praise him in the assembly of the elders.

³³ He turns rivers into a desert,
  springs of water into thirsty ground,
³⁴ a fruitful land into a salty waste,
  because of the wickedness of its inhabitants.
³⁵ He turns a desert into pools of water,
  a parched land into springs of water.
³⁶ And there he lets the hungry live,
  and they establish a town to live in;
³⁷ they sow fields, and plant vineyards,
  and get a fruitful yield.
³⁸ By his blessing they multiply greatly,
  and he does not let their cattle decrease.

³⁹ When they are diminished and brought low
  through oppression, trouble, and sorrow,
⁴⁰ he pours contempt on princes
  and makes them wander in trackless wastes;
⁴¹ but he raises up the needy out of distress,
  and makes their families like flocks.
⁴² The upright see it and are glad;
  and all wickedness stops its mouth.
⁴³ Let those who are wise give heed
   to these things,
  and consider the steadfast love of the LORD.

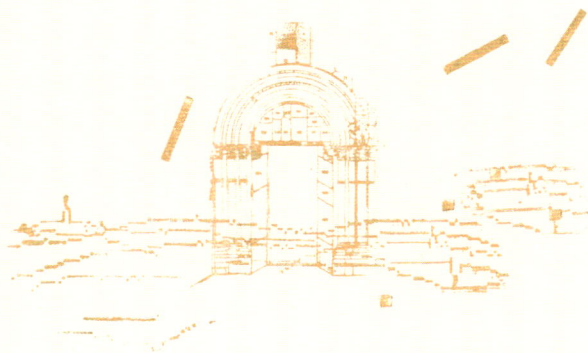

Psalm 108

A Song. A Psalm of David.

My heart is steadfast, O God,
  my heart is steadfast;
  I will sing and make melody.
  Awake, my soul!
² Awake, O harp and lyre!
  I will awake the dawn.
³ I will give thanks to you, O LORD,
   among the peoples,
  and I will sing praises to you
   among the nations.
⁴ For your steadfast love is higher
   than the heavens,
  and your faithfulness reaches to the clouds.

⁵ Be exalted, O God, above the heavens,
  and let your glory be over all the earth.
⁶ Give victory with your right hand,
   and answer me,
  so that those whom you love may be rescued.

⁷ God has promised in his sanctuary:
  "With exultation I will divide up Shechem,
   and portion out the Vale of Succoth.
⁸ Gilead is mine; Manasseh is mine;
   Ephraim is my helmet;
   Judah is my scepter.
⁹ Moab is my washbasin;
   on Edom I hurl my shoe;
   over Philistia I shout in triumph."

¹⁰ Who will bring me to the fortified city?
  Who will lead me to Edom?
¹¹ Have you not rejected us, O God?
  You do not go out, O God, with our armies.
¹² O grant us help against the foe,
  for human help is worthless.
¹³ With God we shall do valiantly;
  it is he who will tread down our foes.

Psalm 109

To the leader: Of David. A Psalm.

Do not be silent, O God of my praise.
² For wicked and deceitful mouths
   are opened against me,
  speaking against me with lying tongues.
³ They beset me with words of hate,
  and attack me without cause.
⁴ In return for my love they accuse me,
  even while I make prayer for them.

^m Cn: Heb *sea*
ⁿ Cn: Heb *fools*
^o Heb Mss Gk Syr: MT lacks
  my heart is steadfast
^p Compare 57.8: Heb *also
  my soul*
^q Or *in his holiness*
^r Syr: Heb *I prayer*

III Thanksgiving
IV Confidence
I Lament

5 So they reward me evil for good,
  and hatred for my love.

6 They say, "Appoint a wicked man against him;
  let an accuser stand on his right.
7 When he is tired, let him be found guilty;
  let his prayer be counted as sin.
8 May his days be few;
  may another seize his position.
9 May his children be orphans,
  and his wife a widow.
10 May his children wander about and beg;
  may they be driven out of the
    ruins they inhabit.
11 May the creditor seize all that he has;
  may strangers plunder the fruits of his toil.
12 May there be no one to do him a kindness,
  nor anyone to pity his orphaned children.
13 May his posterity be cut off;
  may his name be blotted out in
    the second generation.
14 May the iniquity of his father be
    remembered before the LORD,
  and do not let the sin of his
    mother be blotted out.
15 Let them be before the LORD continually,
  and may his memory be cut off
    from the earth.
16 For he did not remember to show kindness,
  but pursued the poor and needy
  and the brokenhearted to their death.
17 He loved to curse; let curses come on him.
  He did not like blessing; may it
    be far from him.
18 He clothed himself with cursing as his coat,
  may it soak into his body like water,
  like oil into his bones.
19 May it be like a garment that he
    wraps around himself,
  like a belt that he wears every day."

20 May that be the reward of my
    accusers from the LORD,
  of those who speak evil against my life.
21 But you, O LORD my Lord,
  act on my behalf for your name's sake;
  because your steadfast love is good,
    deliver me.
22 For I am poor and needy,
  and my heart is pierced within me.
23 I am gone like a shadow at evening;
  I am shaken off like a locust.
24 My knees are weak through fasting;
  my body has become gaunt.

s Heb lacks They say
t Gk: Heb and seek
u Gn: Heb fathers
v Gk: Heb their
w Gk: Heb They have risen
  up and have been put to
  shame
x Another reading is in holy
  splendor
y Gn: Heb the dew of your
  youth
z Or forever, a rightful king
  by my edict

VII Royal.

25 I am an object of scorn to my accusers;
  when they see me, they shake their heads.

26 Help me, O LORD my God!
  Save me according to your steadfast love.
27 Let them know that this is your hand;
  you, O LORD, have done it.
28 Let them curse, but you will bless.
  Let my assailants be put to shame;
  may your servant be glad.
29 May my accusers be clothed with dishonor;
  may they be wrapped in their own
    shame as in a mantle.
30 With my mouth I will give great
    thanks to the LORD;
  I will praise him in the midst of the throng.
31 For he stands at the right hand of the needy,
  to save them from those who would
    condemn them to death.

VII **Psalm 110**

Of David. A Psalm.

The LORD says to my lord,
  "Sit at my right hand
until I make your enemies your footstool."

2 The LORD sends out from Zion
  your mighty scepter.
  Rule in the midst of your foes.
3 Your people will offer themselves willingly
  on the day you lead your forces
  on the holy mountains.
  From the womb of the morning,
    like dew, your youth will come to you.
4 The LORD has sworn and will not
    change his mind,
  "You are a priest forever according to
    the order of Melchizedek."

5 The Lord is at your right hand;
  he will shatter kings on the day of his wrath.
6 He will execute judgment among the nations,
  filling them with corpses;
  he will shatter heads
    over the wide earth.
7 He will drink from the stream by the path;
  therefore he will lift up his head.

Psalm 111

Praise the LORD!
I will give thanks to the LORD with
    my whole heart,
    in the company of the upright,
    in the congregation.
2 Great are the works of the LORD,
    studied by all who delight in them.
3 Full of honor and majesty is his work,
    and his righteousness endures forever.
4 He has gained renown by his wonderful deeds;
    the LORD is gracious and merciful.
5 He provides food for those who fear him;
    he is ever mindful of his covenant.
6 He has shown his people the
    power of his works,
    in giving them the heritage of the nations.
7 The works of his hands are faithful and just;
    all his precepts are trustworthy.
8 They are established forever and ever,
    to be performed with faithfulness
    and uprightness.
9 He sent redemption to his people;
    he has commanded his covenant forever.
    Holy and awesome is his name.
10 The fear of the LORD is the beginning
    of wisdom;
    all those who practice it have
    a good understanding.
    His praise endures forever.

Psalm 112

Praise the LORD!
    Happy are those who fear the LORD,
    who greatly delight in his commandments.
2 Their descendants will be mighty in the land;
    the generation of the upright will be blessed.
3 Wealth and riches are in their houses,
    and their righteousness endures forever.
4 They rise in the darkness as a
    light for the upright;
    they are gracious, merciful, and righteous.
5 It is well with those who deal
    generously and lend,
    who conduct their affairs with justice.
6 For the righteous will never be moved;
    they will be remembered forever.
7 They are not afraid of evil tidings;
    their hearts are firm, secure in the LORD.
8 Their hearts are steady, they will not be afraid;
    in the end they will look in

    triumph on their foes.
9 They have distributed freely, they
    have given to the poor;
    their righteousness endures forever;
    their horn is exalted in honor.
10 The wicked see it and are angry;
    they gnash their teeth and melt away;
    the desire of the wicked comes to nothing.

Psalm 113

Praise the LORD!
    Praise, O servants of the LORD;
    praise the name of the LORD.

2 Blessed be the name of the LORD
    from this time on and forevermore.
3 From the rising of the sun to its setting
    the name of the LORD is to be praised.
4 The LORD is high above all nations,
    and his glory above the heavens.

5 Who is like the LORD our God,
    who is seated on high,
6 who looks far down
    on the heavens and the earth?
7 He raises the poor from the dust,
    and lifts the needy from the ash heap,
8 to make them sit with princes,
    with the princes of his people.
9 He gives the barren woman a home,
    making her the joyous mother of children.
    Praise the LORD!

Psalm 114

When Israel went out from Egypt,
    the house of Jacob from a people
    of strange language,
2 Judah became God's sanctuary,
    Israel his dominion.

3 The sea looked and fled;
    Jordan turned back.
4 The mountains skipped like rams,
    the hills like lambs.

5 Why is it, O sea, that you flee?
    O Jordan, that you turn back?
6 O mountains, that you skip like rams?
    O hills, like lambs?

a Gk Syr: Heb them
b Heb his

11 Hymn
v wisdom

7 Tremble, O earth, at the presence of the LORD,
    at the presence of the God of Jacob,
8 who turns the rock into a pool of water,
    the flint into a spring of water.

Psalm 115

Not to us, O LORD, not to us, but to
    your name give glory,
    for the sake of your steadfast love
    and your faithfulness.
2 Why should the nations say,
    "Where is their God?"

3 Our God is in the heavens;
    he does whatever he pleases.
4 Their idols are silver and gold,
    the work of human hands.
5 They have mouths, but do not speak;
    eyes, but do not see.
6 They have ears, but do not hear;
    noses, but do not smell.
7 They have hands, but do not feel;
    feet, but do not walk;
    they make no sound in their throats.
8 Those who make them are like them;
    so are all who trust in them.

9 O Israel, trust in the LORD!
    He is their help and their shield.
10 O house of Aaron, trust in the LORD!
    He is their help and their shield.
11 You who fear the LORD, trust in the LORD!
    He is their help and their shield.

12 The LORD has been mindful of us;
        he will bless us;
        he will bless the house of Israel;
        he will bless the house of Aaron;
13 he will bless those who fear the LORD,
    both small and great.

14 May the LORD give you increase,
    both you and your children.
15 May you be blessed by the LORD,
    who made heaven and earth.

16 The heavens are the LORD's heavens,
    but the earth he has given to human beings.
17 The dead do not praise the LORD,
    nor do any that go down into silence.
18 But we will bless the LORD
    from this time on and forevermore.
    Praise the LORD!

11 Hymn
111 Thanksgiving

Psalm 116

I love the LORD, because he has heard
    my voice and my supplications.
2 Because he inclined his ear to me,
    therefore I will call on him as long as I live.
3 The snares of death encompassed me;
    the pangs of Sheol laid hold on me;
    I suffered distress and anguish.
4 Then I called on the name of the LORD:
    "O LORD, I pray, save my life!"

5 Gracious is the LORD, and righteous;
    our God is merciful.
6 The LORD protects the simple;
    when I was brought low, he saved me.
7 Return, O my soul, to your rest,
    for the LORD has dealt bountifully with you.

8 For you have delivered my soul from death,
    my eyes from tears,
    my feet from stumbling.
9 I walk before the LORD
    in the land of the living.
10 I kept my faith, even when I said,
    "I am greatly afflicted";
11 I said in my consternation,
    "Everyone is a liar."

12 What shall I return to the LORD
    for all his bounty to me?
13 I will lift up the cup of salvation
    and call on the name of the LORD,
14 I will pay my vows to the LORD
    in the presence of all his people.
15 Precious in the sight of the LORD
    is the death of his faithful ones.
16 O LORD, I am your servant;
    I am your servant, the child of
        your serving girl.
    You have loosed my bonds.
17 I will offer to you a thanksgiving sacrifice
    and call on the name of the LORD.
18 I will pay my vows to the LORD
    in the presence of all his people,
19 in the courts of the house of the LORD,
    in your midst, O Jerusalem.
    Praise the LORD!

Psalm 117

Praise the LORD, all you nations!
    Extol him, all you peoples!
2 For great is his steadfast love toward us,
    and the faithfulness of the
        LORD endures forever.
Praise the LORD!

Psalm 118

O give thanks to the LORD, for he is good;
    his steadfast love endures forever!

2 Let Israel say,
    "His steadfast love endures forever."
3 Let the house of Aaron say,
    "His steadfast love endures forever."
4 Let those who fear the LORD say,
    "His steadfast love endures forever."

5 Out of my distress I called on the LORD;
    the LORD answered me and set me
        in a broad place.
6 With the LORD on my side I do not fear.
    What can mortals do to me?
7 The LORD is on my side to help me;
    I shall look in triumph on
        those who hate me.
8 It is better to take refuge in the LORD
    than to put confidence in mortals.
9 It is better to take refuge in the LORD
    than to put confidence in princes.

10 All nations surrounded me;
    in the name of the LORD I cut them off!
11 They surrounded me, surrounded me
        on every side;
    in the name of the LORD I cut them off!
12 They surrounded me like bees;
    they blazed like a fire of thorns;
    in the name of the LORD I cut them off!
13 I was pushed hard, so that I was falling,
    but the LORD helped me.
14 The LORD is my strength and my might;
    he has become my salvation.

15 There are glad songs of victory in the
        tents of the righteous:
16 "The right hand of the LORD does valiantly;
    the right hand of the LORD is exalted;
    the right hand of the LORD does valiantly."
17 I shall not die, but I shall live,
    and recount the deeds of the LORD.
18 The LORD has punished me severely,
    but he did not give me over to death.

19 Open to me the gates of righteousness,
    that I may enter through them
    and give thanks to the LORD.

20 This is the gate of the LORD;
    the righteous shall enter through it.

21 I thank you that you have answered me
    and have become my salvation.
22 The stone that the builders rejected
    has become the chief cornerstone.
23 This is the LORD's doing;
    it is marvelous in our eyes.
24 This is the day that the LORD has made;
    let us rejoice and be glad in it.
25 Save us, we beseech you, O LORD!
    O LORD, we beseech you, give us success!

26 Blessed is the one who comes in
        the name of the LORD.
    We bless you from the house of the LORD.
27 The LORD is God,
    and he has given us light.
    Bind the festal procession with branches,
    up to the horns of the altar.

28 You are my God, and I will give thanks to you;
    you are my God, I will extol you.

29 O give thanks to the LORD, for he is good,
    for his steadfast love endures forever.

Psalm 119

Happy are those whose way is blameless,
    who walk in the law of the LORD.
2 Happy are those who keep his decrees,
    who seek him with their whole heart,
3 who also do no wrong,
    but walk in his ways.
4 You have commanded your precepts
    to be kept diligently.
5 O that my ways may be steadfast
    in keeping your statutes!
6 Then I shall not be put to shame,
    having my eyes fixed on all your
        commandments.
7 I will praise you with an upright heart,
    when I learn your righteous ordinances.

b Gk Heb were extinguished
d Gk Syr Jerome: Heb You pushed me hard
e Or in him
f Or Blessed in the name of the Lord is the one who comes
g Meaning of Heb uncertain

ii Hymn
iii Thanksgiving
v Wisdom

8 I will observe your statutes;
   do not utterly forsake me.

9 How can young people keep their way pure?
   By guarding it according to your word.
10 With my whole heart I seek you;
   do not let me stray from your
      commandments.
11 I treasure your word in my heart,
   so that I may not sin against you.
12 Blessed are you, O LORD;
   teach me your statutes.
13 With my lips I declare
   all the ordinances of your mouth.
14 I delight in the way of your decrees
   as much as in all riches.
15 I will meditate on your precepts,
   and fix my eyes on your ways.
16 I will delight in your statutes;
   I will not forget your word.

17 Deal bountifully with your servant,
   so that I may live and observe your word.
18 Open my eyes, so that I may behold
   wondrous things out of your law.
19 I live as an alien in the land;
   do not hide your commandments from me.
20 My soul is consumed with longing
   for your ordinances at all times.
21 You rebuke the insolent, accursed ones,
   who wander from your commandments;
22 take away from me their scorn and contempt,
   for I have kept your decrees.
23 Even though princes sit plotting against me,
   your servant will meditate on your statutes.
24 Your decrees are my delight,
   they are my counselors.

25 My soul clings to the dust;
   revive me according to your word.
26 When I told of my ways, you answered me;
   teach me your statutes.
27 Make me understand the ways of your precepts,
   and I will meditate on your wondrous works.
28 My soul melts away for sorrow;
   strengthen me according to your word.
29 Put false ways far from me;
   and graciously teach me your law.
30 I have chosen the way of faithfulness;
   I set your ordinances before me.
31 I cling to your decrees, O LORD;
   let me not be put to shame.
32 I run the way of your commandments,
   for you enlarge my understanding.

33 Teach me, O LORD, the way of your statutes,
   and I will observe it to the end.
34 Give me understanding, that I may
      keep your law
   and observe it with my whole heart.
35 Lead me in the path of your commandments,
   for I delight in it.
36 Turn my heart to your decrees,
   and not to selfish gain.
37 Turn my eyes from looking at vanities;
   give me life in your ways.
38 Confirm to your servant your promise,
   which is for those who fear you.
39 Turn away the disgrace that I dread,
   for your ordinances are good.
40 See, I have longed for your precepts;
   in your righteousness give me life.

41 Let your steadfast love come to me, O LORD,
   your salvation according to your promise.
42 Then I shall have an answer for those
      who taunt me,
   for I trust in your word.
43 Do not take the word of truth utterly
      out of my mouth,
   for my hope is in your ordinances.
44 I will keep your law continually,
   forever and ever.
45 I shall walk at liberty,
   for I have sought your precepts.
46 I will also speak of your decrees before kings,
   and shall not be put to shame;
47 I find my delight in your commandments,
   because I love them.
48 I revere your commandments, which I love,
   and I will meditate on your statutes.

49 Remember your word to your servant,
   in which you have made me hope.
50 This is my comfort in my distress,
   that your promise gives me life.
51 The arrogant utterly deride me,
   but I do not turn away from your law.
52 When I think of your ordinances from of old,
   I take comfort, O LORD.
53 Hot indignation seizes me because
      of the wicked,
   those who forsake your law.
54 Your statutes have been my songs
   wherever I make my home.
55 I remember your name in the night, O LORD,
   and keep your law.
56 This blessing has fallen to me,
   for I have kept your precepts.

57 The LORD is my portion;
    I promise to keep your words.
58 I implore your favor with all my heart;
    be gracious to me according to your promise.
59 When I think of your ways,
    I turn my feet to your decrees;
60 I hurry and do not delay
    to keep your commandments.
61 Though the cords of the wicked ensnare me,
    I do not forget your law.
62 At midnight I rise to praise you,
    because of your righteous ordinances.
63 I am a companion of all who fear you,
    of those who keep your precepts.
64 The earth, O LORD, is full of
        your steadfast love;
    teach me your statutes.

65 You have dealt well with your servant,
    O LORD, according to your word.
66 Teach me good judgment and knowledge,
    for I believe in your commandments.
67 Before I was humbled I went astray,
    but now I keep your word.
68 You are good and do good;
    teach me your statutes.
69 The arrogant smear me with lies,
    but with my whole heart
        I keep your precepts.
70 Their hearts are fat and gross,
    but I delight in your law.
71 It is good for me that I was humbled,
    so that I might learn your statutes.
72 The law of your mouth is better to me
    than thousands of gold and silver pieces.

73 Your hands have made and fashioned me;
    give me understanding that I may learn
        your commandments.
74 Those who fear you shall see me and rejoice,
    because I have hoped in your word.
75 I know, O LORD, that your judgments are right,
    and that in faithfulness
        you have humbled me.
76 Let your steadfast love become my comfort
    according to your promise to your servant.
77 Let your mercy come to me, that I may live;
    for your law is my delight.
78 Let the arrogant be put to shame,
    because they have subverted me with guile;
    as for me, I will meditate on your precepts.
79 Let those who fear you turn to me,
    so that they may know your decrees.
80 May my heart be blameless in your statutes,

so that I may not be put to shame.

81 My soul languishes for your salvation;
    I hope in your word.
82 My eyes fail with watching for your promise;
    I ask, "When will you comfort me?"
83 For I have become like a wineskin
        in the smoke,
    yet I have not forgotten your statutes.
84 How long must your servant endure?
    When will you judge those
        who persecute me?
85 The arrogant have dug pitfalls for me;
    they flout your law.
86 All your commandments are enduring;
    I am persecuted without cause; help me!
87 They have almost made an end of me on earth;
    but I have not forsaken your precepts.
88 In your steadfast love spare my life,
    so that I may keep the decrees
        of your mouth.

89 The LORD exists forever;
    your word is firmly fixed in heaven.
90 Your faithfulness endures to all generations;
    you have established the earth,
        and it stands fast.
91 By your appointment they stand today,
    for all things are your servants.
92 If your law had not been my delight,
    I would have perished in my misery.
93 I will never forget your precepts,
    for by them you have given me life.
94 I am yours; save me,
    for I have sought your precepts.
95 The wicked lie in wait to destroy me,
    but I consider your decrees.
96 I have seen a limit to all perfection,
    but your commandment is
        exceedingly broad.

97 Oh, how I love your law!
    It is my meditation all day long.
98 Your commandment makes me wiser
        than my enemies,
    for it is always with me.
99 I have more understanding than
        all my teachers,
    for your decrees are my meditation.
100 I understand more than the aged,
    for I keep your precepts.
101 I hold back my feet from every evil way,
    in order to keep your word.
102 I do not turn away from your ordinances,

for you have taught me.

103 How sweet are your words to my taste,
sweeter than honey to my mouth!

104 Through your precepts I get understanding;
therefore I hate every false way.

105 Your word is a lamp to my feet
and a light to my path.

106 I have sworn an oath and confirmed it,
to observe your righteous ordinances.

107 I am severely afflicted;
give me life, O LORD, according to your word.

108 Accept my offerings of praise, O LORD,
and teach me your ordinances.

109 I hold my life in my hand continually,
but I do not forget your law.

110 The wicked have laid a snare for me,
but I do not stray from your precepts.

111 Your decrees are my heritage forever;
they are the joy of my heart.

112 I incline my heart to perform your statutes
forever, to the end.

113 I hate the double-minded,
but I love your law.

114 You are my hiding place and my shield;
I hope in your word.

115 Go away from me, you evildoers,
that I may keep the commandments
of my God.

116 Uphold me according to your promise,
that I may live,
and let me not be put to shame in my hope.

117 Hold me up, that I may be safe
and have regard for your statutes continually.

118 You spurn all who go astray
from your statutes;
for their cunning is in vain.

119 All the wicked of the earth you count as dross;
therefore I love your decrees.

120 My flesh trembles for fear of you,
and I am afraid of your judgments.

121 I have done what is just and right;
do not leave me to my oppressors.

122 Guarantee your servant's well-being;
do not let the godless oppress me.

123 My eyes fail from watching for your salvation,
and for the fulfillment of your
righteous promise.

124 Deal with your servant according to
your steadfast love,
and teach me your statutes.

125 I am your servant; give me understanding,

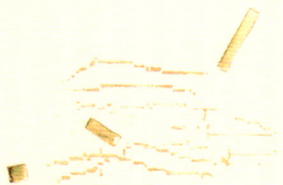

*b Gk Jerome: Meaning of
Heb uncertain*

so that I may know your decrees.

126 It is time for the LORD to act,
for your law has been broken.

127 Truly I love your commandments
more than gold, more than fine gold.

128 Truly I direct my steps by all your precepts;
I hate every false way.

129 Your decrees are wonderful;
therefore my soul keeps them.

130 The unfolding of your words gives light;
it imparts understanding to the simple.

131 With open mouth I pant,
because I long for your commandments.

132 Turn to me and be gracious to me,
as is your custom toward those who
love your name.

133 Keep my steps steady according
to your promise,
and never let iniquity have dominion over me.

134 Redeem me from human oppression,
that I may keep your precepts.

135 Make your face shine upon your servant,
and teach me your statutes.

136 My eyes shed streams of tears
because your law is not kept.

137 You are righteous, O LORD,
and your judgments are right.

138 You have appointed your decrees
in righteousness
and in all faithfulness.

139 My zeal consumes me
because my foes forget your words.

140 Your promise is well tried,
and your servant loves it.

141 I am small and despised,
yet I do not forget your precepts.

142 Your righteousness is an everlasting
righteousness,
and your law is the truth.

143 Trouble and anguish have come upon me,
but your commandments are my delight.

144 Your decrees are righteous forever;
give me understanding that I may live.

145 With my whole heart I cry;
answer me, O LORD.
I will keep your statutes.

146 I cry to you; save me,
that I may observe your decrees.

147 I rise before dawn and cry for help;
I put my hope in your words.

148 My eyes are awake before each

watch of the night,
that I may meditate on your promise.

149 In your steadfast love hear my voice;
O LORD, in your justice preserve my life.

150 Those who persecute me with evil
purpose draw near;
they are far from your law.

151 Yet you are near, O LORD,
and all your commandments are true.

152 Long ago I learned from your decrees
that you have established them forever.

153 Look on my misery and rescue me,
for I do not forget your law.

154 Plead my cause and redeem me;
give me life according to your promise.

155 Salvation is far from the wicked,
for they do not seek your statutes.

156 Great is your mercy, O LORD;
give me life according to your justice.

157 Many are my persecutors and my adversaries,
yet I do not swerve from your decrees.

158 I look at the faithless with disgust,
because they do not keep your commands.

159 Consider how I love your precepts;
preserve my life according to
your steadfast love.

160 The sum of your word is truth;
and every one of your righteous
ordinances endures forever.

161 Princes persecute me without cause,
but my heart stands in awe of your words.

162 I rejoice at your word
like one who finds great spoil.

163 I hate and abhor falsehood,
but I love your law.

164 Seven times a day I praise you
for your righteous ordinances.

165 Great peace have those who love your law;
nothing can make them stumble.

166 I hope for your salvation, O LORD,
and I fulfill your commandments.

167 My soul keeps your decrees;
I love them exceedingly.

168 I keep your precepts and decrees,
for all my ways are before you.

169 Let my cry come before you, O LORD;
give me understanding according
to your word.

170 Let my supplication come before you;
deliver me according to your promise.

171 My lips will pour forth praise,

because you teach me your statutes.

172 My tongue will sing of your promise,
for all your commandments are right.

173 Let your hand be ready to help me,
for I have chosen your precepts.

174 I long for your salvation, O LORD,
and your law is my delight.

175 Let me live that I may praise you,
and let your ordinances help me.

176 I have gone astray like a lost sheep;
seek out your servant,
for I do not forget your commandments.

Psalm 120

A Song of Ascents.

In my distress I cry to the LORD,
that he may answer me:

2 "Deliver me, O LORD,
from lying lips,
from a deceitful tongue."

3 What shall be given to you?
And what more shall be done to you,
you deceitful tongue?

4 A warrior's sharp arrows,
with glowing coals of the broom tree!

5 Woe is me, that I am an alien in Meshech,
that I must live among the tents of Kedar.

6 Too long have I had my dwelling
among those who hate peace.

7 I am for peace;
but when I speak,
they are for war.

Psalm 121

A Song of Ascents.

I lift up my eyes to the hills—
from where will my help come?

2 My help comes from the LORD,
who made heaven and earth.

3 He will not let your foot be moved;
he who keeps you will not slumber.

4 He who keeps Israel
will neither slumber nor sleep.

5 The LORD is your keeper;
the LORD is your shade at your right hand.

6 The sun shall not strike you by day,
nor the moon by night.

7 The LORD will keep you from all evil;
    he will keep your life.
8 The LORD will keep
    your going out and your coming in
    from this time on and forevermore.

VIII Psalm 122

A Song of Ascents. Of David.

I was glad when they said to me,
    "Let us go to the house of the LORD!"
2 Our feet are standing
    within your gates, O Jerusalem.

3 Jerusalem – built as a city
    that is bound firmly together.
4 To it the tribes go up,
    the tribes of the LORD,
    as was decreed for Israel,
    to give thanks to the name of the LORD.
5 For there the thrones for judgment
    were set up,
    the thrones of the house of David.

6 Pray for the peace of Jerusalem:
    "May they prosper who love you.
7 Peace be within your walls,
    and security within your towers."
8 For the sake of my relatives and friends
    I will say, "Peace be within you."
9 For the sake of the house of the LORD our God,
    I will seek your good.

Psalm 123

A Song of Ascents.

To you I lift up my eyes,
    O you who are enthroned in the heavens!
2 As the eyes of servants
    look to the hand of their master,
    as the eyes of a maid
    to the hand of her mistress,
    so our eyes look to the LORD our God,
    until he has mercy upon us.

3 Have mercy upon us, O LORD,
    have mercy upon us,
    for we have had more than
    enough of contempt.
4 Our soul has had more than its fill
    of the scorn of those who are at ease,
    of the contempt of the proud.

VIII Zion Songs
I Lament
III Thanksgiving
IV Confidence

III Psalm 124

A Song of Ascents. Of David.

If it had not been the LORD who
    was on our side
    – let Israel now say –
2 if it had not been the LORD who
    was on our side,
    when our enemies attacked us,
3 then they would have swallowed us up alive,
    when their anger was kindled against us;
4 then the flood would have swept us away,
    the torrent would have gone over us;
5 then over us would have gone
    the raging waters.

6 Blessed be the LORD,
    who has not given us
    as prey to their teeth.
7 We have escaped like a bird
    from the snare of the fowlers;
    the snare is broken,
    and we have escaped.

8 Our help is in the name of the LORD,
    who made heaven and earth.

IV Psalm 125

A Song of Ascents.

Those who trust in the LORD are like
    Mount Zion,
    which cannot be moved, but abides forever.
2 As the mountains surround Jerusalem,
    so the LORD surrounds his people,
    from this time on and forevermore.
3 For the scepter of wickedness shall not rest
    on the land allotted to the righteous,
    so that the righteous might not stretch out
    their hands to do wrong.
4 Do good, O LORD, to those who are good,
    and to those who are upright in their hearts.
5 But those who turn aside to their
    own crooked ways
    the LORD will lead away with evildoers.
    Peace be upon Israel!

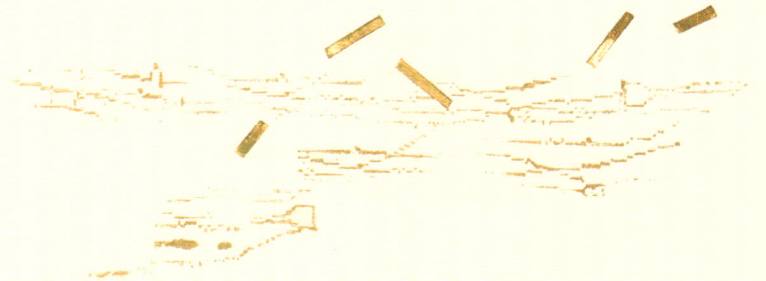

Psalm 126

A Song of Ascents.

When the LORD restored the fortunes of Zion,
 we were like those who dream.
2 Then our mouth was filled with laughter,
 and our tongue with shouts of joy;
 then it was said among the nations,
 "The LORD has done great things for them."
3 The LORD has done great things for us,
 and we rejoiced.

4 Restore our fortunes, O LORD,
 like the watercourses in the Negeb.
5 May those who sow in tears
 reap with shouts of joy.
6 Those who go out weeping,
 bearing the seed for sowing,
 shall come home with shouts of joy,
 carrying their sheaves.

Psalm 127

A Song of Ascents. Of Solomon.

Unless the LORD builds the house,
 those who build it labor in vain.
Unless the LORD guards the city,
 the guard keeps watch in vain.
2 It is in vain that you rise up early
 and go late to rest,
 eating the bread of anxious toil;
 for he gives sleep to his beloved.

3 Sons are indeed a heritage from the LORD,
 the fruit of the womb a reward.
4 Like arrows in the hand of a warrior
 are the sons of one's youth.
5 Happy is the man who has
 his quiver full of them.
He shall not be put to shame
 when he speaks with his enemies in the gate.

Psalm 128

A Song of Ascents.

Happy is everyone who fears the LORD,
 who walks in his ways.
2 You shall eat the fruit of the
 labor of your hands;
 you shall be happy, and it shall
 go well with you.

3 Your wife will be like a fruitful vine
 within your house;
 your children will be like olive shoots
 around your table.
4 Thus shall the man be blessed
 who fears the LORD.

5 The LORD bless you from Zion.
 May you see the prosperity of Jerusalem
 all the days of your life.
6 May you see your children's children.
 Peace be upon Israel!

Psalm 129

A Song of Ascents.

Often have they attacked me from my youth"
 — let Israel now say —
2 "often have they attacked me from my youth,
 yet they have not prevailed against me.
3 The plowers plowed on my back;
 they made their furrows long."
4 The LORD is righteous;
 he has cut the cords of the wicked.
5 May all who hate Zion
 be put to shame and turned backward.
6 Let them be like the grass on the housetops
 that withers before it grows up,
7 with which reapers do not fill their hands
 or binders of sheaves their arms,
8 while those who pass by do not say,
 "The blessing of the LORD be upon you!
 We bless you in the name of the LORD!"

Psalm 130

A Song of Ascents.

Out of the depths I cry to you, O LORD.
2 Lord, hear my voice!
Let your ears be attentive
 to the voice of my supplications!

3 If you, O LORD, should mark iniquities,
 Lord, who could stand?
4 But there is forgiveness with you,
 so that you may be revered.

5 I wait for the LORD, my soul waits,
 and in his word I hope;

t Or brought back those
 who returned to Zion
j Or for he provides for his
 beloved during sleep

i Lament
v Wisdom
iii Thanksgiving

⁶ my soul waits for the Lord
more than those who watch for the morning,
more than those who watch for the morning.

⁷ O Israel, hope in the LORD!
For with the LORD there is steadfast love,
and with him is great power to redeem.
⁸ It is he who will redeem Israel
from all its iniquities.

^{IV} Psalm 131

A Song of Ascents. Of David.

O LORD, my heart is not lifted up,
my eyes are not raised too high;
I do not occupy myself with things
too great and too marvelous for me.
² But I have calmed and quieted my soul,
like a weaned child with its mother;
my soul is like the weaned child
that is with me.^k

³ O Israel, hope in the LORD
from this time on and forevermore.

^{VI} Psalm 132

A Song of Ascents.

O LORD, remember in David's favor
all the hardships he endured;
² how he swore to the LORD
and vowed to the Mighty One of Jacob,
³ "I will not enter my house
or get into my bed;
⁴ I will not give sleep to my eyes
or slumber to my eyelids,
⁵ until I find a place for the LORD,
a dwelling place for the
Mighty One of Jacob."

⁶ We heard of it in Ephrathah;
we found it in the fields of Jaar.
⁷ "Let us go to his dwelling place;
let us worship at his footstool."

⁸ Rise up, O LORD, and go to your resting place,
you and the ark of your might.
⁹ Let your priests be clothed with righteousness,
and let your faithful shout for joy.
¹⁰ For your servant David's sake
do not turn away the face
of your anointed one.

^k **or** *my soul within me is
like a weaned child*

¹¹ The LORD swore to David a sure oath
from which he will not turn back:
"One of the sons of your body
I will set on your throne.
¹² If your sons keep my covenant
and my decrees that I shall teach them,
their sons also, forevermore,
shall sit on your throne."

¹³ For the LORD has chosen Zion;
he has desired it for his habitation:
¹⁴ "This is my resting place forever;
here I will reside, for I have desired it.
¹⁵ I will abundantly bless its provisions;
I will satisfy its poor with bread.
¹⁶ Its priests I will clothe with salvation,
and its faithful will shout for joy.
¹⁷ There I will cause a horn
to sprout up for David;
I have prepared a lamp for my anointed one.
¹⁸ His enemies I will clothe with disgrace,
but on him, his crown will gleam."

^V Psalm 133

A Song of Ascents.

How very good and pleasant it is
when kindred live together in unity!
² It is like the precious oil on the head,
running down upon the beard,
on the beard of Aaron,
running down over the collar of his robes.
³ It is like the dew of Hermon,
which falls on the mountains of Zion.
For there the LORD ordained his blessing,
life forevermore.

^{VI} Psalm 134

A Song of Ascents.

Come, bless the LORD, all you servants
of the LORD,
who stand by night in the house of the LORD!
² Lift up your hands to the holy place,
and bless the LORD.

³ May the LORD, maker of heaven and earth,
bless you from Zion.

Psalm 135

Praise the LORD!
  Praise the name of the LORD;
    give praise, O servants of the LORD,
2 you that stand in the house of the LORD,
    in the courts of the house of our God.
3 Praise the LORD, for the LORD is good;
    sing to his name, for he is gracious.
4 For the LORD has chosen Jacob for himself,
    Israel as his own possession.

5 For I know that the LORD is great;
    our Lord is above all gods.
6 Whatever the LORD pleases he does,
    in heaven and on earth,
    in the seas and all deeps.
7 He it is who makes the clouds rise
      at the end of the earth;
    he makes lightnings for the rain
    and brings out the wind from
      his storehouses.

8 He it was who struck down the
      firstborn of Egypt,
    both human beings and animals:
9 he sent signs and wonders
    into your midst, O Egypt,
    against Pharaoh and all his servants.
10 He struck down many nations
    and killed mighty kings—
11 Sihon, king of the Amorites,
    and Og, king of Bashan,
    and all the kingdoms of Canaan—
12 and gave their land as a heritage,
    a heritage to his people Israel.

13 Your name, O LORD, endures forever,
    your renown, O LORD, throughout all ages.
14 For the LORD will vindicate his people,
    and have compassion on his servants.

15 The idols of the nations are silver and gold,
    the work of human hands.
16 They have mouths, but they do not speak;
    they have eyes, but they do not see;
17 they have ears, but they do not hear,
    and there is no breath in their mouths.
18 Those who make them
    and all who trust them
    shall become like them.

19 O house of Israel, bless the LORD!
    O house of Aaron, bless the LORD!

20 O house of Levi, bless the LORD!
    You that fear the LORD, bless the LORD!
21 Blessed be the LORD from Zion,
    he who resides in Jerusalem.
    Praise the LORD!

Psalm 136

O give thanks to the LORD, for he is good,
    for his steadfast love endures forever.
2 O give thanks to the God of gods,
    for his steadfast love endures forever.
3 O give thanks to the Lord of lords,
    for his steadfast love endures forever;

4 who alone does great wonders,
    for his steadfast love endures forever;
5 who by understanding made the heavens,
    for his steadfast love endures forever;
6 who spread out the earth on the waters,
    for his steadfast love endures forever;
7 who made the great lights,
    for his steadfast love endures forever;
8 the sun to rule over the day,
    for his steadfast love endures forever;
9 the moon and stars to rule over the night,
    for his steadfast love endures forever;

10 who struck Egypt through their firstborn,
    for his steadfast love endures forever;
11 and brought Israel out from among them,
    for his steadfast love endures forever;
12 with a strong hand and an outstretched arm,
    for his steadfast love endures forever;
13 who divided the Red Sea in two,
    for his steadfast love endures forever;
14 and made Israel pass through the midst of it,
    for his steadfast love endures forever;
15 but overthrew Pharaoh and his army
      in the Red Sea,
    for his steadfast love endures forever;
16 who led his people through the wilderness,
    for his steadfast love endures forever;
17 who struck down great kings,
    for his steadfast love endures forever;
18 and killed famous kings,
    for his steadfast love endures forever;
19 Sihon, king of the Amorites,
    for his steadfast love endures forever;
20 and Og, king of Bashan,
    for his steadfast love endures forever;
21 and gave their land as a heritage,
    for his steadfast love endures forever;

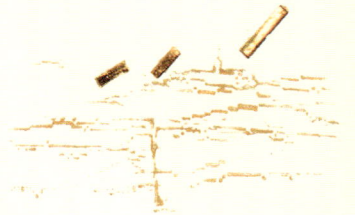

m
Or *Sea of Reeds*

IX Historical

²² a heritage to his servant Israel,
　　for his steadfast love endures forever.

²³ It is he who remembered us in our low estate,
　　for his steadfast love endures forever;

²⁴ and rescued us from our foes,
　　for his steadfast love endures forever;

²⁵ who gives food to all flesh,
　　for his steadfast love endures forever.

²⁶ O give thanks to the God of heaven,
　　for his steadfast love endures forever.

Psalm 137

¹ By the rivers of Babylon —
　　there we sat down and there we wept
　　when we remembered Zion.
² On the willowsⁿ there
　　we hung up our harps.
³ For there our captors
　　asked us for songs,
　　and our tormentors asked for mirth, saying,
　　"Sing us one of the songs of Zion!"

⁴ How could we sing the LORD's song
　　in a foreign land?
⁵ If I forget you, O Jerusalem,
　　let my right hand wither!
⁶ Let my tongue cling to the roof of my mouth,
　　if I do not remember you,
　　if I do not set Jerusalem
　　above my highest joy.

⁷ Remember, O LORD, against the Edomites
　　the day of Jerusalem's fall,
　　how they said, "Tear it down! Tear it down!
　　Down to its foundations!"
⁸ O daughter Babylon, you devastator!^o
　　Happy shall they be who pay you back
　　what you have done to us!
⁹ Happy shall they be who take your little ones
　　and dash them against the rock!

Psalm 138

Of David.

¹ I give you thanks, O LORD, with my
　　whole heart;^p
　　before the gods I sing your praise;
² I bow down toward your holy temple
　　and give thanks to your name for your

ⁿ Or *poplars*
^o Or *you who are devastated*
^p Cn: Heb *you have exalted your word above all your name*
^q Syr Compare Gk Tg: Heb *you made me arrogant in my soul with strength*

I Lament
III Thanksgiving
V Wisdom

steadfast love and your faithfulness;
　　for you have exalted your name
　　and your word
　　above everything.^p
³ On the day I called, you answered me,
　　you increased my strength of soul.^q

⁴ All the kings of the earth shall
　　praise you, O LORD,
　　for they have heard the words
　　of your mouth.
⁵ They shall sing the ways of the LORD,
　　for great is the glory of the LORD.
⁶ For though the LORD is high,
　　he regards the lowly;
　　but the haughty he perceives from far away.

⁷ Though I walk in the midst of trouble,
　　you preserve me against the
　　wrath of my enemies;
　　you stretch out your hand,
　　and your right hand delivers me.
⁸ The LORD will fulfill his purpose for me;
　　your steadfast love, O LORD, endures forever.
　　Do not forsake the work of your hands.

Psalm 139

To the leader. Of David. A Psalm.

¹ O LORD, you have searched me and known me.
² You know when I sit down and when I rise up;
　　you discern my thoughts from far away.
³ You search out my path and my lying down,
　　and are acquainted with all my ways.
⁴ Even before a word is on my tongue,
　　O LORD, you know it completely.
⁵ You hem me in, behind and before,
　　and lay your hand upon me.
⁶ Such knowledge is too wonderful for me;
　　it is so high that I cannot attain it.

⁷ Where can I go from your spirit?
　　Or where can I flee from your presence?
⁸ If I ascend to heaven, you are there;
　　if I make my bed in Sheol, you are there.
⁹ If I take the wings of the morning
　　and settle at the farthest limits of the sea,
¹⁰ even there your hand shall lead me,
　　and your right hand shall hold me fast.
¹¹ If I say, "Surely the darkness shall cover me,
　　and the light around me become night,"
¹² even the darkness is not dark to you;
　　the night is as bright as the day,
　　for darkness is as light to you.

¹³ For it was you who formed my inward parts;
  you knit me together in my mother's womb.
¹⁴ I praise you, for I am fearfully
    and wonderfully made.
  Wonderful are your works;
  that I know very well.
¹⁵ My frame was not hidden from you,
  when I was being made in secret,
  intricately woven in the depths of the earth.
¹⁶ Your eyes beheld my unformed substance.
  In your book were written
    all the days that were formed for me,
    when none of them as yet existed.
¹⁷ How weighty to me are your thoughts, O God!
  How vast is the sum of them!
¹⁸ I try to count them – they are more
    than the sand;
  I come to the end – I am still with you.

¹⁹ O that you would kill the wicked, O God,
  and that the bloodthirsty would
    depart from me –
²⁰ those who speak of you maliciously,
  and lift themselves up against you for evil!
²¹ Do I not hate those who hate you, O LORD?
  And do I not loathe those who rise
    up against you?
²² I hate them with perfect hatred;
  I count them my enemies.
²³ Search me, O God, and know my heart;
  test me and know my thoughts.
²⁴ See if there is any wicked way in me,
  and lead me in the way everlasting.

Psalm 140

To the leader. A Psalm of David.

Deliver me, O LORD, from evildoers;
  protect me from those who are violent,
² who plan evil things in their minds
  and stir up wars continually.
³ They make their tongue sharp as a snake's,
  and under their lips is the venom
    of vipers.   *Selah*

⁴ Guard me, O LORD, from the hands
    of the wicked;
  protect me from the violent
  who have planned my downfall.
⁵ The arrogant have hidden a trap for me,
  and with cords they have spread a net,
  along the road they have set
    snares for me.   *Selah*

⁶ I say to the LORD, "You are my God;
  give ear, O LORD, to the voice
    of my supplications."
⁷ O LORD, my Lord, my strong deliverer,
  you have covered my head in
    the day of battle.
⁸ Do not grant, O LORD, the desires
    of the wicked;
  do not further their evil plot.   *Selah*

⁹ Those who surround me lift up their heads;
  let the mischief of their lips
    overwhelm them!
¹⁰ Let burning coals fall on them!
  Let them be flung into pits, no more to rise!
¹¹ Do not let the slanderer be established
    in the land;
  let evil speedily hunt down the violent!

¹² I know that the LORD maintains the
    cause of the needy,
  and executes justice for the poor.
¹³ Surely the righteous shall give
    thanks to your name;
  the upright shall live in your presence.

Psalm 141

A Psalm of David.

I call upon you, O LORD; come quickly to me;
  give ear to my voice when I call to you.
² Let my prayer be counted as
    incense before you,
  and the lifting up of my hands as
    an evening sacrifice.

³ Set a guard over my mouth, O LORD;
  keep watch over the door of my lips.
⁴ Do not turn my heart to any evil,
  to busy myself with wicked deeds
  in company with those who work iniquity;
  do not let me eat of their delicacies.

⁵ Let the righteous strike me;
  let the faithful correct me.
  Never let the oil of the wicked
    anoint my head,
  for my prayer is continually against
    their wicked deeds.
⁶ When they are given over to those
    who shall condemn them,
  then they shall learn that my
    words were pleasant.

RSB
Psalm 140:11

ᵗ Or *I awake*
ˢ Cn: Meaning of Heb
  uncertain
ᵗ Heb *hurtful*
ᵘ Or *the ancient way*
  Compare Jer 6.16
ᵛ Or *they have spread cords
  as a net*
ʷ Heb adds *they are
  exalted*
ˣ Cn Compare Gk: Heb
  *those who surround me
  are uplifted in head*; Heb
  divides verses 8 and 9
  differently
ʸ Gk: Meaning of Heb
  uncertain
ᶻ Cn: Heb *for continually
  and my prayer*

1 Lament

7 Like a rock that one breaks apart
   and shatters on the land,
   so shall their bones be strewn
   at the mouth of Sheol.

8 But my eyes are turned toward you,
   O GOD, my Lord;
   in you I seek refuge; do not
   leave me defenseless.
9 Keep me from the trap that they
   have laid for me,
   and from the snares of evildoers.
10 Let the wicked fall into their own nets,
   while I alone escape.

Psalm 142

A Maskil of David. When he was in the cave.
A Prayer.

With my voice I cry to the LORD;
   with my voice I make supplication
   to the LORD.
2 I pour out my complaint before him;
   I tell my trouble before him.
3 When my spirit is faint,
   you know my way.

In the path where I walk
   they have hidden a trap for me.
4 Look on my right hand and see ~
   there is no one who takes notice of me;
no refuge remains to me;
   no one cares for me.

5 I cry to you, O LORD;
   I say, "You are my refuge,
   my portion in the land of the living."
6 Give heed to my cry,
   for I am brought very low.

Save me from my persecutors,
   for they are too strong for me.
7 Bring me out of prison,
   so that I may give thanks to your name.
The righteous will surround me,
   for you will deal bountifully with me.

a Meaning of Heb of
  verses 5-7 is uncertain
b One Heb Ms Gk MT *to*
  you I have hidden

I Lament

Psalm 143

A Psalm of David.

Hear my prayer, O LORD;
give ear to my supplications in
your faithfulness;
answer me in your righteousness.

2 Do not enter into judgment with your servant;
   for no one living is righteous before you.

3 For the enemy has pursued me,
   crushing my life to the ground,
   making me sit in darkness like
      those long dead.
4 Therefore my spirit faints within me;
   my heart within me is appalled.

5 I remember the days of old,
   I think about all your deeds,
   I meditate on the works of your hands.
6 I stretch out my hands to you;
   my soul thirsts for you
      like a parched land.   Selah

7 Answer me quickly, O LORD;
   my spirit fails.
Do not hide your face from me,
   or I shall be like those who
   go down to the Pit.
8 Let me hear of your steadfast love
      in the morning,
   for in you I put my trust.
Teach me the way I should go,
   for to you I lift up my soul.

9 Save me, O LORD, from my enemies;
   I have fled to you for refuge.
10 Teach me to do your will,
   for you are my God.
Let your good spirit lead me
   on a level path.

11 For your name's sake, O LORD, preserve my life.
   In your righteousness bring me
      out of trouble.
12 In your steadfast love cut off my enemies,
   and destroy all my adversaries,
   for I am your servant.

Psalm 144

Of David.

Blessed be the LORD, my rock,
who trains my hands for war,
and my fingers for battle;
2 my rock and my fortress,
my stronghold and my deliverer,
my shield, in whom I take refuge,
who subdues the peoples under me.

3 O LORD, what are human beings that
you regard them,
or mortals that you think of them?
4 They are like a breath;
their days are like a passing shadow.

5 Bow your heavens, O LORD, and come down;
touch the mountains so that they smoke.
6 Make the lightning flash and scatter them;
send out your arrows and rout them.
7 Stretch out your hand from on high;
set me free and rescue me from
the mighty waters,
from the hand of aliens,
8 whose mouths speak lies,
and whose right hands are false.

9 I will sing a new song to you, O God;
upon a ten-stringed harp I will play to you,
10 the one who gives victory to kings,
who rescues his servant David.
11 Rescue me from the cruel sword,
and deliver me from the hand of aliens,
whose mouths speak lies,
and whose right hands are false.

12 May our sons in their youth
be like plants full grown,
our daughters like corner pillars,
cut for the building of a palace.
13 May our barns be filled,
with produce of every kind;
may our sheep increase by thousands,
by tens of thousands in our fields,
14 and may our cattle be heavy with young.
May there be no breach in the walls, no exile,
and no cry of distress in our streets.

15 Happy are the people to whom
such blessings fall;
happy are the people whose
God is the LORD.

Psalm 145

Praise. Of David.

I will extol you, my God and King,
and bless your name forever and ever.
2 Every day I will bless you;
and praise your name forever and ever.
3 Great is the LORD, and greatly to be praised;
his greatness is unsearchable.

4 One generation shall laud your
works to another,
and shall declare your mighty acts.
5 On the glorious splendor of your majesty,
and on your wondrous works,
I will meditate.
6 The might of your awesome deeds
shall be proclaimed,
and I will declare your greatness.
7 They shall celebrate the fame of
your abundant goodness,
and shall sing aloud of your righteousness.

8 The LORD is gracious and merciful,
slow to anger and abounding
in steadfast love.
9 The LORD is good to all,
and his compassion is over all
that he has made.

10 All your works shall give thanks
to you, O LORD,
and all your faithful shall bless you.
11 They shall speak of the glory
of your kingdom,
and tell of your power,
12 to make known to all people
your mighty deeds,
and the glorious splendor
of your kingdom.
13 Your kingdom is an everlasting kingdom,
and your dominion endures throughout
all generations.

The LORD is faithful in all his words,
and gracious in all his deeds.
14 The LORD upholds all who are falling,
and raises up all who are bowed down.
15 The eyes of all look to you;
and you give them their food
in due season.
16 You open your hand,
satisfying the desire of every living thing.
17 The LORD is just in all his ways,

c With 18.2 and 2 Sam 22.2:
Heb *my steadfast love*
d Heb Mss Syr Aquila
Jerome MT *my people*
e Heb lacks *in the walls*
f Gk Jerome Syr: Heb *his*
g Heb *his*
h These two lines supplied
by Q Ms Gk Syr

VII Royal
II Hymn

and kind in all his doings.
¹⁸ The LORD is near to all who call on him,
   to all who call on him in truth.
¹⁹ He fulfills the desire of all who fear him;
   he also hears their cry, and saves them.
²⁰ The LORD watches over all who love him,
   but all the wicked he will destroy.

²¹ My mouth will speak the praise
      of the LORD,
   and all flesh will bless his holy
      name forever and ever.

ⁿ Psalm 146

Praise the LORD!
   Praise the LORD, O my soul!
² I will praise the LORD as long as I live;
   I will sing praises to my God
      all my life long.

³ Do not put your trust in princes,
   in mortals, in whom there is no help.
⁴ When their breath departs, they
      return to the earth;
   on that very day their plans perish.

⁵ Happy are those whose help is the
      God of Jacob,
   whose hope is in the LORD their God,
⁶ who made heaven and earth,
   the sea, and all that is in them;
who keeps faith forever;
⁷   who executes justice for the oppressed;
   who gives food to the hungry.

   The LORD sets the prisoners free;
⁸   the LORD opens the eyes of the blind.
The LORD lifts up those who are bowed down;
   the LORD loves the righteous.
⁹ The LORD watches over the strangers;
   he upholds the orphan and the widow,
   but the way of the wicked he brings to ruin.

¹⁰ The LORD will reign forever,
   your God, O Zion, for all generations.
   Praise the LORD!

^j Heb *leas of a person*
   or *prosperity*

n Hymn

ⁿ Psalm 147

Praise the LORD!
   How good it is to sing praises to our God;
      for he is gracious, and a song of
         praise is fitting.
² The LORD builds up Jerusalem;
   he gathers the outcasts of Israel.
³ He heals the brokenhearted,
   and binds up their wounds.
⁴ He determines the number of the stars;
   he gives to all of them their names.
⁵ Great is our LORD, and abundant in power;
   his understanding is beyond measure.
⁶ The LORD lifts up the downtrodden;
   he casts the wicked to the ground.

⁷ Sing to the LORD with thanksgiving;
   make melody to our God on the lyre.
⁸ He covers the heavens with clouds,
   prepares rain for the earth,
   makes grass grow on the hills.
⁹ He gives to the animals their food,
   and to the young ravens when they cry.
¹⁰ His delight is not in the strength of the horse,
   nor his pleasure in the speed of a runner;
¹¹ but the LORD takes pleasure in
      those who fear him,
   in those who hope in his steadfast love.

¹² Praise the LORD, O Jerusalem!
   Praise your God, O Zion!
¹³ For he strengthens the bars of your gates;
   he blesses your children within you.
¹⁴ He grants peace within your borders;
   he fills you with the finest of wheat.
¹⁵ He sends out his command to the earth;
   his word runs swiftly.
¹⁶ He gives snow like wool;
   he scatters frost like ashes.
¹⁷ He hurls down hail like crumbs—
   who can stand before his cold?
¹⁸ He sends out his word, and melts them;
   he makes his wind blow, and the waters flow.
¹⁹ He declares his word to Jacob,
   his statutes and ordinances to Israel.
²⁰ He has not dealt thus with any other nation;
   they do not know his ordinances.
   Praise the LORD!

Psalm 148

Praise the LORD!
Praise the LORD from the heavens;
   praise him in the heights!
2 Praise him, all his angels;
   praise him, all his hosts!

3 Praise him, sun and moon;
   praise him, all you shining stars!
4 Praise him, you highest heavens,
   and you waters above the heavens!

5 Let them praise the name of the LORD,
   for he commanded and they were created.
6 He established them forever and ever;
   he fixed their bounds, which
      cannot be passed.

7 Praise the LORD from the earth,
   you sea monsters and all deeps,
8 fire and hail, snow and frost,
   stormy wind fulfilling his command!

9 Mountains and all hills,
   fruit trees and all cedars!
10 Wild animals and all cattle,
   creeping things and flying birds!

11 Kings of the earth and all peoples,
   princes and all rulers of the earth!
12 Young men and women alike,
   old and young together!

13 Let them praise the name of the LORD,
   for his name alone is exalted;
   his glory is above earth and heaven.
14 He has raised up a horn for his people,
   praise for all his faithful,
   for the people of Israel who are close to him.
Praise the LORD!

Psalm 149

Praise the LORD!
Sing to the LORD a new song,
   his praise in the assembly of the faithful.
2 Let Israel be glad in its Maker;
   let the children of Zion rejoice in their King.
3 Let them praise his name with dancing,
   making melody to him with
      tambourine and lyre.
4 For the LORD takes pleasure in his people;

   he adorns the humble with victory.
5 Let the faithful exult in glory;
   let them sing for joy on their couches.
6 Let the high praises of God be in their throats
   and two-edged swords in their hands,
7 to execute vengeance on the nations
   and punishment on the peoples,
8 to bind their kings with fetters
   and their nobles with chains of iron,
9 to execute on them the judgment decreed.
   This is glory for all his faithful ones.
Praise the LORD!

Psalm 150

Praise the LORD!
Praise God in his sanctuary;
praise him in his
   mighty firmament!
2 Praise him for his mighty deeds;
praise him according to
   his surpassing greatness!

3 Praise him with trumpet sound;
praise him with lute & harp!
4 Praise him with
   tambourine and dance;
praise him with strings & pipe!
5 Praise him with
   clanging cymbals;
praise him with
   loud clashing cymbals!
6 Let everything that breathes
praise the LORD!
Praise the LORD!

Praise the LORD!

Praise the LORD!

Praise the LORD!